ONE DIRECTION
NO LIMITS

Mick O'Shea

CONTENTS

INTRODUCTION

FIVE DREAMS: ONE DIRECTION

> 'I wake up so many mornings feeling so lucky
> and so grateful to be where we are.'
> – Harry

Love it or loathe it, *The X Factor* has given countless hopefuls the chance to stand in front of a panel of judges and reveal their talents – or lack thereof. Once upon a time the only hope an unknown singer had of getting a recording contract was to send off a professionally made demo to record companies – often at great personal expense – and pray that one of the A&R departments might actually give it a listen rather than use it as a doorstop. And again, love him or loathe him, it's thanks to Simon Cowell that the power has been taken away from the record companies and given back to the aspiring artist. Because while not everyone will make it to the televised stages of the competition, each and every applicant is assured of a three-minute shot at the title – regardless of whether they've been educated at prestigious theatre schools, singing for their supper in clubland, or have yet to sing anywhere outside of their bedroom or bathroom with a hairbrush serving as a microphone.

However, where the *X Factor* format differs from how a record company would treat any newly-signed act is that, while a record company would groom and nurture the artist, gaining them gradual exposure through press interviews and various TV shows, the more talented of the *X Factor* hopefuls go straight from auditioning in a nondescript room in front of Simon and the rest of that year's judging panel, to singing in front of a highly-charged studio audience within a matter of weeks, during which time, of course, the minutiae of their lives will have been painstakingly dissected by the media.

The majority of those who apply to *The X Factor* will have undoubtedly watched the previous series and cheered on their respective favourites, all the while believing that they could do better. But, of course, watching from the safety of one's armchair isn't quite the same as walking out onto a stage – especially *The X Factor*'s glitzy, gladiatorial Live Show stage. Comparing the *X Factor* studio to the amphitheatres of Ancient Rome may seem extreme, but the analogy isn't all that far-fetched, because while the finalists don't actually physically compete against each other, they are expected to cope with incredibly stressful televised trials and tribulations, during which time some will lose the fight to conquer their nerves.

Then, having given their all, they have to stand on stage – with the cameras flitting from face to face – as the show's host, Dermot O'Leary, lingers over announcing which acts are going through to next week's show, cranking up the tension levels to the max. And for those acts with the fewest votes, who then have to go head-to-head in the show's 'Final Showdown', it really must seem like a matter of life and death.

'The reason why the fans are so dedicated is because I think they feel like they can really relate to us, like we're the kind of boys that you go to school with – and we are.'
– Harry

Some critics, of course, will argue that *The X Factor* is far more concerned with weekly viewing figures, and claiming the Christmas Number One, than it is with taking care of the eventual winner. Yet, while previous winners have enjoyed varying degrees of success, there's never a shortage of aspiring contestants all anxious to step up to plate, because while it may be a well-worn cliché, hope springs eternal for those who dare to dream.

And oh, how the dream came true for five young hopefuls who entered the 2010 series of *The X Factor* as random individuals, and left it together, ready to forge a path as One Direction.

As the world now knows, despite the quintet falling at the final hurdle, Simon Cowell was waiting in the wings to pick them up again and launch them into the stratosphere, but if you thought you knew everything there was to know about Niall, Zayn, Liam, Louis and Harry, then think again . . .

FIVE DREAMS: ONE DIRECTIO

CHAPTER ONE

JOKER IN THE PACK

Louis William Tomlinson

Place of Birth: Doncaster, South Yorkshire

Date of Birth: 24 December 1991

Star Sign: Capricorn

'I talked a lot from a really young age. I've always been a little bit gobby and not lacking in confidence. Apparently I used to sit in my pushchair and talk to random people and get annoyed when they wouldn't reply. I wasn't a shy boy.'

If – as *X Factor* judge Louis Walsh has claimed – One Direction are the new Take That, then his being the self-confessed joker in the pack makes Louis the Robbie Williams of the band. However, whereas Robbie's green-eyed envy over Gary Barlow receiving more of the spotlight ultimately led to him quitting the band to go it alone, Louis doesn't appear to have a jealous bone in his body, and is totally committed to the One Direction cause. His being a couple of years older than the other boys also allows him to act as their unspoken leader.

While Louis's being born close to Christmas certainly made it a holiday season to remember for his doting parents, Mark and Johannah, it can prove a double-edged sword for most kids, for while they enjoy two bumper paydays in quick succession, the general consensus is that they receive fewer presents than they might have had they been born at any other time of year. Louis, however, looked upon this happenstance as an opportunity to have a full year to focus on what presents he really wanted. And like many boys his age he was fascinated with all things Power Rangers – or *Mighty Morphin*

Power Rangers, as the Super Sentai cartoon characters were originally known. He even admits having actually wanted to be a Power Ranger at one point.

Having watched the latest weekly instalment, he would use his ever-growing collection of Power Rangers action figures to re-enact the show's plotline. 'I was obsessed with Power Rangers,' he revealed in *Dare To Dream*. 'Whenever I was asked what I wanted for Christmas or my birthday I always chose a new Power Rangers toy. The Red Ranger was my favourite. When I met Zayn, I discovered he was mad about them too, and we used to swap notes.'

As Mark and Johannah's family gradually grew, and Louis gained four younger siblings – Charlotte, Félicité, and twins, Daisy and Phoebe – all of them girls, these colour-coded, space-age action men served as a male bastion to protect him from their giggling, girly ways. For though his dad helped to even up the numbers within the Tomlinson household – at least until his parents' separation in 2011 – the pair were at a serious disadvantage. 'When I was growing up there were five women running around [the house], so dad and I had to stick together,' he later joked. 'I suppose in some ways it did teach me about women. I'm certainly not intimidated by them – because I'm used to them.'

> **'I remember one of my teachers saying to me once, when I was fifteen,**
> **"I can tell by your personality that you're going to go on to do big things."'**
> **– Louis**

Back when Louis was four, before his sisters had entered the picture, his parents relocated to Poole in Dorset, and while being uprooted from his familiar surroundings at such an early age would have no doubt proved daunting, living by the sea more than made up for the disruption – the Power Rangers rides in the seaside town's amusement arcades proving the greatest distraction of all. 'What young lad wouldn't love living by the sea and being surrounded by amusements?' he subsequently reflected. 'There was always a lot going on and it was a perfect place for a young kid to be.'

But just as Louis – or 'Boo Bear', to give him his childhood nickname – was beginning to find his feet and make friends at primary school, his mum fell pregnant with his eldest sister, Charlotte, and they elected to return to Doncaster and set up home in the village of Bessacarr. 'I was about six [when Charlotte was born] and I burst into tears because I was so overwhelmed with the whole experience,' he later revealed. 'I was incredibly happy, but I'd been an only child up until then so it was probably a shock to me. It's great having that many siblings [and] all my sisters are amazing, but I would have liked another boy in the house.'

Louis has since revealed how growing up with four younger siblings – regardless of their sex – instilled a yearning in him for a little boy of his own, and that Harry and the other band members constantly tease him over his broodiness. 'I definitely, definitely want kids of my own one day, [and] there is a slight possibility that I might end up with around fifteen to twenty kids if I don't have a son straight away – something to be aware of, I guess, for anyone thinking of marrying me.'

With his dad out at work, and baby Charlotte taking up much of his mum's time, each day after school Louis would be picked up by his devoted grandma, Edna, who'd take him to the park if the weather permitted before taking him back to her house, where granddad Len would be waiting, more often than not with an ice-cream. Indeed, such was Louis's relationship with his grandparents that he spent as much time at their house as he did his own. Sadly, however, while Edna was a huge fan of *The X Factor*, she didn't live to see Louis's subsequent success on the show.

Unlike the vast majority of his peers, Louis has said that he not only enjoyed his time at school, but actually misses it: 'It was more of a social thing, and I was the one trying to make people laugh,' he says in *One Direction: Forever Young*. 'The teachers either really didn't like me or got on with me. I remember one of my RE teachers saying to me once, when I was fifteen, "I can tell by your personality that you're going to go on to do big things." I went back to Doncaster recently and went to see his [the RE teacher's] class and say hello, and he reminded me of it.'

Indeed, such was his enjoyment that he also took great interest in which secondary school he'd be attending, as he subsequently explained: 'There were two schools in my local area, and the one I really wanted to go to was called Hayfield. I didn't get in,

though, and ended up going to another school called Hall Cross. It was fine there but I never really settled, and although I made a couple of really good friends, I just wasn't very happy.'

Imagine his parents' consternation, then, when Louis pulled a face when he was subsequently offered a place at Hayfield. 'That was quite hard because I was now thirteen and everyone else had been there for quite a while and they all knew each other,' Louis explained. 'I was the new kid, so the first few weeks getting to know everyone were tough.'

Fortunately for Mark and Johannah, their pernickety son eventually found his feet. So much so that he now admits to being glad he made the move, as Hayfield was the setting for some of his happiest childhood memories. However, many of these memorable experiences occurred outside of the classroom. 'I remember lots of stories from the parties I went to during sixth form, some of which were pretty crazy,' he confessed in *Dare To Dream*. 'One party, I'd had a few drinks and I missed my lift home and needed a place to stay so the obvious solution was to walk to the airport with my friends and sleep there.'

Waking up at the airport with a hangover, however, was the least of Louis's problems, as his party lifestyle meant that, while he passed eight out of the eleven GCSEs he sat, he ended up failing the first year of his A-levels. Hayfield's strict policy meant he wouldn't be able re-sit them, and as a result of his errant ways he had to return to Hall Cross and start his A-levels from scratch. At Hayfield he'd been studying Psychology, English Literature, PE and IT, but ended up dropping English Lit at Hall Cross because, by his own admission, things were getting a bit too much. He would subsequently admit to having lost interest in his A-levels simply because he's unable to put his mind to something if his heart isn't in it.

'It was a blow to me, but thankfully I was seventeen and happy to make new friends. Even though I felt a bit of an idiot because I was a year older than everyone else,' he said of his experience. 'I soon felt like I fitted in. Also, I was the only one in my year who could drive, which was quite a nice position to be in as it meant I could ferry people

around. It was great being able to drive everyone around in my 1.2 Clio. It had alloy wheels and central locking and was my pride and joy. It was really my Nan's car, but it kind of ended up being mine because she never used it.'

Needless to say, while Louis enjoyed partying with his pals, when it came to donning his chauffeur's cap he much preferred escorting girls. 'I won't lie, I was a bit of a flirt at school and I always liked girls' company,' he subsequently admitted. 'I really liked this girl called Beth, and we were friends for about six months, then we started seeing each other when I was about fifteen. We stayed together for two years and two months and we got on so well, it was really nice. Later on it all started to get a bit too intense for that age, so we split up.'

While it's fair to say that Beth is very happy to have dated one of the most famous young men ever to hail from Doncaster, one cannot help but wonder how many of the girls who were in Louis's class falsely brag about how they once enjoyed a snog with him

behind the bike sheds, or a smooch at one of the school discos. Of course, back when he was plain Louis Tomlinson no one was really interested in his thoughts about the opposite sex, but in a candid interview with *Teen Now* magazine back in April 2011, he revealed that while he could be a 'bit of a joker', he was also something of a romantic at heart. However, he is careful to keep things on a certain level. 'You have to get the banter in there, too,' he said, 'otherwise you scare the girl away.'

If the girl in question wasn't scared away by his unique choice of attire, of course – 'I'd probably wear purple chinos, they sound disgusting but they look cool, and a polo or T-shirt and a cardigan.' His being old-fashioned meant they needn't worry if they came out without their purse, and when asked if he would take the girl's number at the end of the evening, Louis tactfully replied: 'Of course, although it would depend on how the date goes. If it wasn't a great date, I might let her down slowly – I hate guys who ignore girls.'

And for those curious to know what boxes a prospective girlfriend might have to tick to get up close and personal? 'Someone who is loyal and has a sense of humour, and is kind-hearted, too. Oh, and if they're tidy, that would be good, because I'm not!'

It was at Hayfield that Louis took his first excursion into music when h[e]
friends' invitation to join their band, The Rogue, as singer – even thougl[i]
heard him sing! 'We used to practice once a week even though we didn't [
and we used to play a lot of Green Day and think we were rock'n'roll. At th[e]
term we used to perform a song for our year group. I really enjoyed performing and yet
I never had the courage to do a whole school assembly because I was intimidated, so it's
weird to think that I've ended up performing on stage in front of thousands.'

After eighteen months or so, The Rogue decided they wanted to try another singer,
but Louis was far from disheartened as his best friend Stan, who was the guitarist in the
band, left with him – they even took the band name with them. 'We used to do acoustic
gigs, but it was more for fun than anything, and we never expected to make it big,' Louis
says today. 'I just loved the feeling of performing to an audience.'

Louis's artistic talents weren't solely restricted to his singing in a school band,
however, for when Daisy and Phoebe – who were getting occasional bits of work as
television extras on account of their being identical twins – were invited to appear in the ITV series *Fat Friends*, their big brother landed himself a walk-on part. (Of course, the next time Daisy and Phoebe were in the spotlight with Louis came when he made a surprise visit to Doncaster in the week leading up to *The X*

> 'I remember lots of stories from the parties I went to during sixth form, some of which were pretty crazy.'
> – Louis

Factor semi-final and called in at his old school, Willow Primary, where the girls were
enrolled. And the previous week the six-year-olds had been granted special permission
by the show's producers and allowed into the studio to watch Louis when One Direction
performed 'Summer Of '69' and 'You Are So Beautiful' on Rock Week, when the show's
contestants performed guitar-driven anthems.)

Now that he'd been bitten by the acting bug, Louis started attending an acting school,
got himself an agent, and landed similar 'blink-and-you'll-miss-him' roles in the 2006
ITV film *If I Had You*, and BBC One's long-running, gritty school drama, *Waterloo Road*.
However, the highlight of Louis's acting career to date undoubtedly came at Hall Cross
when the school was staging *Grease* – which also, of course, happens to be his favourite
film – as that year's Christmas musical, and he landed the role of Danny Zuko. It was the
first musical he'd auditioned for, so to land the lead male role was especially pleasing.
So much so, that he's subsequently posted a couple of video clips from the play – of
him performing 'Summer Nights' and 'Alone At The Drive-In Movie' – on YouTube.

'That was on the same day that that I had an interview for a Christmas job at Toys
R Us. My mum picked me up from my interview to make sure I went to the audition
because she knew I was in two minds about it,' Louis explained. 'Luckily it went well
and I was so happy when I was told I'd got the role of Danny. I still get emotional when
I watch the video back because it was such a special time for me. I felt proud of landing
the lead and I put everything into it.' The chills were indeed electrifying. So much so,
in fact, that Louis says a career in acting is something he will 'definitely think about
pursuing later on'. Directioners can breathe easy, however, because he currently has

only one thing on his mind: 'For now it's all about the band. I won't stop until we're absolutely massive.'

Needless to say, mum Johannah was in the audience to watch Louis strut his T-bird stuff in the school play – little realising that the next time she'd be watching her boy on stage would be a far grander occasion. Indeed, when the media began taking an interest in One Direction following the opening live show, a bewildered Johannah told her local Doncaster newspaper, *The Star*, how she'd seen her only boy go from performing in front of 200 parents to performing in front of an estimated television audience of 14.8 million in less than twelve months.

Having told the paper how much she and the rest of the family were missing Louis while he was away on *The X Factor*, she went on to reveal her emotions upon seeing Louis on the opening live show: 'It was brilliant – I could hardly remember the performance. We watched a recording of it again when we got home and that was easier to take in because we weren't nervous then because it wasn't live.'

When Louis wasn't going in front of the microphone or the camera, he could be found manning the till at Doncaster Rovers FC's Keepmoat Stadium, which by his own admission had more to do with the free food than what was happening out on the pitch. Another double-bonus job came when he found work at the local Vue Cinema, as in essence he got paid while watching all the new films for free. He'd initially been placed on three months' probation, but owing to his fondness for partying with his mates – and his subsequent tendency to call in sick – three months had to be extended to seven and a half months. 'I think they [the Vue's management] quite liked me and probably wanted to keep me on, but they wouldn't commit to giving me a full-time job,' he said. 'In the end, it was actually *The X Factor* that ended the job for me. When I first applied for the show I had an audition on a day when I was supposed to be working, so I got a friend to cover for me. He forgot and didn't turn up – but it was my responsibility. It was the last straw and I got the boot.'

The audition Louis is referring to was for the 2009 series of *The X Factor*. In hindsight, he'd have been better off turning up for work at the cinema as he fell at the first hurdle. However, rather than slink away and forget his dreams of becoming a pop star, Louis simply knuckled down and spent the intervening twelve months taking singing lessons and brushing up on his technique. By his own admission, all he wanted was to get through to the Judges' Houses stage, to be told whether he was any good or not. 'I wanted to have that experience so I could say I'd done it and not always wonder what it would have been like,' he explained. 'I thought about it all the time, so when I got the letter inviting me to auditions I was so happy.'

However, though he was ecstatic at being given a second shot, he purposely chose to keep his intentions about going for *X Factor* glory again a guarded secret because it was all about proving his worth as a singer to himself. It's fair to say that he also kept his cards close to his chest in order to avoid having his confidence knocked by the more fair-weathered of his friends, who'd enjoyed hearing of his failure the first time round and would have relished a repeat performance. For despite his steely determination to succeed, the thought of having to trudge home a second time with his tail between

'I won't lie,
I was a bit of
a flirt at school
and I always liked
girls' company.'
– Louis

his legs and have his ambitions ridiculed once again inevitably chipped away at his already fraying nerves.

'I waited quite a while in the holding room, [and] then my number was called. Just before you go on stage this guy counts you down and it's like, "Three, two, one – on you go!"' he explained. 'As soon as I saw the audience and the judges, the adrenaline kicked in and my mouth went dry.'

His fraying nerves weren't helped when Simon called a halt midway through his rendition of Scouting For Girls' 'Elvis Ain't Dead' and asked him to sing something else. Thankfully, Simon was rather more impressed with his second song choice – 'Hey There Delilah' by the Plain White T's. Louis also got the thumbs up from Louis Walsh and guest judge Nicole Scherzinger, but all three felt the need to tell him they were concerned about his confidence. However, it wasn't a lack of confidence that had marred his performance, but rather his lack of sleep, as he'd only managed to grab a couple of hours of shut-eye in the car en route to the Manchester MEN Arena, where the auditions were being staged. Needless to say, he made sure he got a good night's rest before heading down to London for the nerve-shredding second stage of *The X Factor* – the culling process that is Bootcamp – at the end of July.

As with every other year the Bootcamp process was staged at Wembley Arena. But if Louis was under any illusion that getting three yeses from the judges back in Manchester was going to curry any favour here, then said illusions were instantly dispelled by Louis Walsh, who told the assembled hopefuls that show business is tough, and that to survive in

'I wanted to have that experience so I could say I'd done it and not always wonder what it would have been like. I thought about it all the time, so when I got the letter inviting me to auditions I was so happy.'

– Louis

show business they would need to be equally tough. 'It was all a bit scary,' he later revealed. 'Suddenly everything seemed so real and we all had to fight to prove that we deserved to be there and get through to the Judges' Houses. I'd been having so much fun with the excitement of it all, but now there was everything to sing for.'

Despite the experience being somewhat overwhelming, Louis said that he still had the wherewithal to recognise what was going on around him: 'When I got to Bootcamp I could tell that some people were already trying to play the game, but I don't actually remember that many of the finalists apart from Zayn and Aiden [Grimshaw], because I [made] friends with them. There was a massive hype about Cher [Lloyd] even then, and even though I didn't speak to them much I remembered Harry and Liam well, because I saw them and thought, "You are definitely getting through."'

The first day of Bootcamp was taken up by Simon Cowell and Louis Walsh splitting the 211 acts into their respective categories: Boys, Girls, Groups, and Over-25s. As their fellow judges were absent – Dannii Minogue was on maternity leave, and Cheryl Cole was still recovering from malaria following her recent visit to Tasmania – the show's producers had decided against having the acts perform in front of a live studio audience. This would prove something of a double-edged sword for the contestants, because while performing in front of a live audience would have proved daunting to all but the most fearless, winning over the audience would significantly improve one's chances of swaying the judges.

Aside from befriending Zayn and Aiden, Louis got pally with another hopeful called John Adams, with whom he spent much of his spare time rehearsing: 'We knew we didn't have the strongest voices of all the people there,' he admitted. 'But we didn't want to come out of the competition thinking, "What if I had rehearsed a bit more?"'

Having received vocal coaching from Savan Kotecha, Louis was asked to perform Michael Jackson's 1988 US Number One 'Man In The Mirror' (as were Zayn, Niall, Liam and Harry). At the end of that first day, Cowell and Walsh then went about paring down the acts to 108, and what a feeling it must have been for Louis – and indeed for all five boys – when he was given the nod to say that he'd done enough. Day Two, of course, was far more relaxed simply because, while the 27 acts in each category were shown the dance moves to their respective song by the show's creative director, Brian Friedman, the culling wouldn't resume until the following day. 'Brian told us that we were going to be learning a proper routine. My mouth just fell open. I had no idea what I'd be like, but I was willing to give it a go,'

For Louis, Zayn, Liam, Niall and Harry – as well as the other 103 hopefuls – Day Three was 'D-Day': the day when they'd either be one step closer to seeing their dreams come to fruition, or else see those dreams crushed – at least for another twelve months, until the auditions for next series rolled around. Each act was asked to choose from a list of 40 songs and Louis opted for 'Make You Feel My Love', which was written by Bob Dylan, and appeared on the American folk rock legend's 1997 album, *Time Out Of Mind*, but has since been covered by an array of artists ranging from Neil Diamond to Kelly Clarkson.

Sadly for Louis, Simon Cowell and company were left unmoved by his performance. Though he was naturally upset, he was at least honest enough to admit that he knew he hadn't done as much as he could have on the day. Indeed, he was more surprised that Harry and Liam hadn't gone through.

CHAPTER TWO

REAL GOOD-LOOKING BOY

Zain Javadd Malik

Place of Birth: East Bowling, West Yorkshire

Date of Birth: 12 January 1993

Star Sign: Capricorn

'I don't mean to be a bighead, but I was quite popular at school.
I was a bit of a bad boy and I used to mess about and have a laugh.
I did well all the same and passed eleven GCSEs with high grades.
I remember my drama teacher telling me that if I carried on and worked
hard I could really make something of myself, but I thought she
probably said that to everyone so I took it with a pinch of salt.'

With his olive complexion and smouldering matinee-idol looks, Zain – or 'Zayn' as he's more commonly known – was always going to be serious eye candy for the girls he encountered, but since finding fame with One Direction on *The X Factor*, he's inadvertently become the ultimate pin-up of pin-ups. 'I think it's nice to have support from anyone out there, but for them to be female is always better!' he revealed to *Teen Now* magazine. 'To be called a heartthrob is obviously flattering and I appreciate it, but it's a bit weird.'

Like Louis, Zayn grew up in a house dominated by females, and as the majority of his cousins were also girls he was brought up surrounded by a strong female influence. 'That definitely had an effect on my personality and I was much more sensitive when I was growing up because I was around women all the time. I also think as a result I understand women more than the average man does, to be honest,' he explained. 'I was with my mum and sisters through their ups and downs, so there were times when I needed to lock myself in my room to escape, and I can still pick up on things like that now.'

The times when he locked himself in his room were probably spent poring over comic books – and Zayn is still a fan. 'I'm into comic books,' he admits sheepishly. 'I used to collect them when I was younger, which is quite a geeky thing to do, I think.'

And, again like Louis, Zayn has developed a real bond with all his sisters. While being in One Direction means he can't spend as much quality time with them as he might like, they know they can always count on his continued support. However, that doesn't mean to say he's a pushover. 'I look after my sisters, but I'm also firm and I tell them if they need to go and clean their rooms or whatever, and they listen to me,' he revealed in *Dare To Dream*. 'I think I'm pretty good to them too. Whenever I have a bit of money I buy them presents, and I always look out for them.'

Yet another thing Zayn has in common with Louis – aside from their both being Capricorns and having a shared love of Power Rangers – is that he is Yorkshire born and bred. His olive skin tone comes from his mixed-race parentage, as his mother Tricia is English, while his dad Yaser is a British-Pakistani. 'I've always felt like I've had the best of both worlds from my parents. In terms of heritage, music, tastes, everything,' he revealed to *Teen Now*. 'I'm very close to my dad, he's like my best friend . . . but I am pretty much a mummy's boy. She does everything for me!'

'I was a bit of a handful when I was a kid because I was quite hyperactive. If I got the tiniest bit of sugar in me I'd be bouncing off the walls and jumping from one room to the next.'
– Zayn

While Bradford has also long been home to a multicultural community, being of mixed race wasn't without its inherent problems, as Zayn himself subsequently explained: 'I didn't fit in [at] my first two schools because I was the only mixed heritage kid in my class. My granddad Mohammed was born in Pakistan and my dad was born in England, [while] my mum's dad was Irish and her mum was English, so I'm Irish/English/Asian, which is quite a mix.'

His elder sister Doniya was also experiencing prejudice because of their ethnic origins, so it was decided to move them to a school where they wouldn't be left feeling like the odd ones out. 'Our new school was a lot more mixed, so I felt like I fitted in much better.' And an unexpected, but nonetheless pleasing aspect of changing schools was the attention he started receiving from the girls in his class: '[They] all wanted to know who this new kid was, and that's when I became cool.'

Though Zayn saw himself as 'Mr. Cool' at Tong High School, by his own admission he was something of a live wire at home. 'I was a bit of a handful when I was a kid because I was quite hyperactive,' he said. 'If I got the tiniest bit of sugar in me I'd be bouncing off the walls and jumping from one room to the next. Even in the house my mum used to have to put me in my pram and make me stay there because I was so full-on all the time.

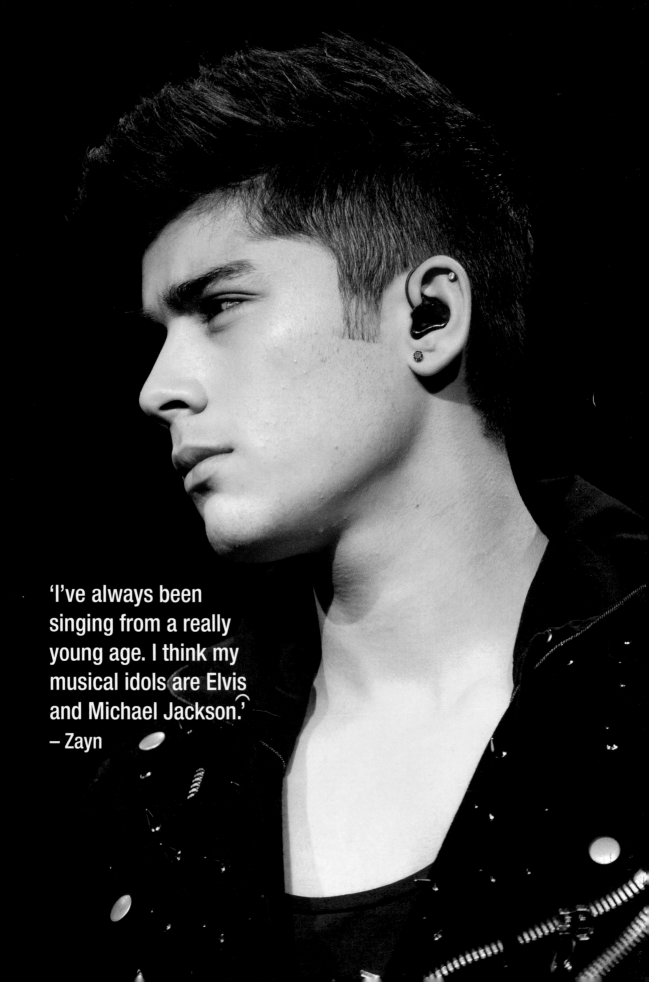

'I've always been singing from a really young age. I think my musical idols are Elvis and Michael Jackson.'
– Zayn

'I'm very close to my dad, he's like my best friend . . . but I am pretty much a mummy's boy. She does everything for me!'
– Zayn

I had endless energy, but at the same time I was quite reserved and if things bothered me I'd keep them bottled up.'

One way of channelling his seemingly limitless energy – as well as ensuring he remained popular with the girls in school – was to join the school's drama class. And yet another similarity with Louis is that his first acting role came in *Grease*, but as he had yet to grow to his full height, he was deemed too small to carry off being a fully-fledged 'T-Bird', so the teacher took poetic license and created a new role for Zayn, so he could play a junior member of the musical's famous teenage gang. 'I was really short for my age up until I went to sixth form,' he explained. '[Then] all of a sudden in the summer holidays and sixth form I grew absolutely loads. I remember being hungry all the time and having pains in my legs. My mum didn't know what was wrong with me, but I guess they must have been growing pains. It was almost like I went to bed one night and woke up tall.'

Following on from his 'Young T-Bird' role, Zayn got a significant part in *Arabian Nights*, before landing the role of Bugsy in *Bugsy Malone*. 'I absolutely loved being on stage and becoming somebody else,' he enthused. 'I found being a character really liberating and I used to get such an adrenaline rush from acting.'

Perhaps not surprisingly, Zayn neglected to mention the private performances he used to put on for his family. 'I have quite a few videos of him singing as a little boy but he's banned me from showing anyone,' his mum Tricia recently revealed. 'My favourite is him singing "I Believe I Can Fly" wearing a green dressing gown.'

Aside from blossoming on the school stage, Zayn was something of a star pupil in the classroom – especially his English classes, as he had a reading ability by far and away above the norm. 'My reading age was about the same as an eighteen-year-old's from the age I was eight,' he revealed. 'I ended up taking my English GCSE a year early and got an A. I wanted to re-sit and get an A*, but they [the teachers] wouldn't let me.' Zayn loved English so much that he has said, if it hadn't been for *The X Factor*, 'I would have been going to uni to do an English degree because I wanted to be an English teacher.' He'd surely have had all the girls fighting to be teacher's pet!

Zayn had a similarly innate talent for art, having clearly inherited the genes from his artist dad. 'One of my hobbies is drawing,' he revealed. 'I've been drawing since I was like five, six years old. I just used to draw cartoons – my favourite thing to draw was Casper as a child, and then I kind of went from there, started drawing Power Rangers and other things. What I like most about drawing is that it gives you a chance to take some time out and kind of express yourself without having to say too much.' However, his creative flair was no help when it came to Maths: '[The subject] never made any sense to me as I couldn't stand it,' he said.

> 'I've always felt like I've had the best of both worlds from my parents. In terms of heritage, music, tastes, everything.'
> – Zayn

Somewhat surprisingly, singing was very much a secondary consideration while Zayn was at school, and he said he only joined the school choir because his music teacher badgered him into it. Of course, as One Direction's star steadily rose on *The X Factor* live shows, it was inevitable that Zayn's teachers and fellow pupils at Tong High avidly followed his progress. Indeed, in the week leading up to Rock Week the school held a 'Zayn Celebration Day'.

The *Bradford Telegraph & Argus* – having championed another home-grown talent in Gareth Gates, runner-up to winner Will Young in the first series of *Pop Idol* back in 2002 – was on hand to witness the exciting proceedings, and the school's deputy head, Steve Gates, told the paper that Zayn was 'a model student who excelled in all the performing arts subjects, one of the specialist subjects here at Tong. He was always a star performer in all the school productions so it was no surprise when Simon Cowell threw him his big chance.'

The paper also called in at Zayn's first school, Lower Fields Primary, where head teacher John Edwards said that everyone was very excited and pleased with Zayn's progress so far. 'Even those of us who don't normally watch the programme have a level of interest this year,' he said. 'I remember he was a nice young man, hard-working, and I remember in particular his leading role in the Year Six leavers' play.'

Like many aspiring child actors, Zayn began developing his own style by experimenting with his clothes, which unfortunately didn't always go according to plan. 'I had a few dodgy haircuts over the years and I shaved my head a few times when I was younger, and also had slits in my eyebrows,' he sheepishly revealed. 'I thought I was proper "gangsta" being into R&B and rap, and I thought they made me look hard. I also went through a really chavvy phase where I wore jogger bottoms and hoodies all the time. Again, I thought I looked great, but looking back probably not . . .'

While Zayn had doubts about some of his riskier sartorial experiments, the girls at school certainly didn't share his misgivings, and those who had their eye on him would – in that time-honoured tradition – send a friend to ask if he'd go out with them. And while he says he didn't get his first 'real' girlfriend until he was fifteen or so, his first kiss came several years earlier. 'I had my first kiss when I was about nine or ten. I was so short that I had to get a brick and put it up against a wall so I could stand on it and reach the girl's face. I remember thinking, "Eww, I just kissed a girl, that was horrible!" It was only a peck, but I was paranoid that people would find out. I thought people would know just from looking at me that I'd kissed someone.'

Despite his being able to have the pick of any girl in school – or indeed any other school – Zayn purposely shied away from getting seriously involved with anyone, and only had two or three proper girlfriends during that time. 'I wouldn't say I've got a specific type when it comes to girls. I've become a lot less shallow as I've got older,' he subsequently reflected. 'Personality is very important to me now. Someone can be the best-looking person in the world, but if they're boring there's nothing worse. You have to have something to stimulate you mentally.'

> **'One of my hobbies is drawing. I've been drawing since I was like five, six years old. I just used to draw cartoons.'**
> **– Zayn**

Having led such a sheltered pre-*X Factor* existence, there seemed to be no stopping him once he was on the show. Aside from the much-publicised four-month romance with fellow finalist Rebecca Ferguson, he also enjoyed a brief fling with Geneva Lane from Belle Amie, as well as a rumoured tryst with Cher Lloyd. And nor did he content himself with the girls from the 2010 series, as the following year he was caught canoodling with eighteen-year-old Perrie Edwards from Little Mix on the set of the video shoot for that year's *X Factor* charity single, 'Wishing On A Star', on which One Direction had been invited to perform. The romance was deemed more newsworthy than Little Mix's triumph in *The X Factor* final, but unfortunately for Zayn, Perrie's commitments in the wake of all-girl group's victory over Marcus Collins meant she had to put the band before her new beau. 'There are no boys for us,' the feisty Geordie told reporters, 'we're going to be like nuns.'

However, it seemed Zayn was a habit Perrie couldn't quite shake, and following One Direction's return from their Australasia tour, the pair set the rumour mill creaking by going online to discuss their clandestine date at the cinema. 'Just went to see avengers assemble and it was #boring. Good night though! xD,' Perrie tweeted upon her return home, while Zayn responded: 'yeah tonight was fun lets do it again sometime ;) x x.' And the following morning he was at it again: 'So its true. Persistence pays off. X :).'

While it won't come as much of a surprise to learn that Zayn was an avid fan of *The X Factor*, unlike most auditionees he was also something of an avid collector of the

'I had my first kiss when I was about nine or ten. I was so short that I had to get a brick and put it up against a wall so I could stand on it and reach the girl's face.'
– Zayn

show's application forms, having sent for a copy in both 2008 and 2009 before finally plucking up the courage to actually put pen to paper and pop the form in the post. 'My music teacher [the fantastic Mrs. Fox] suggested that I went for it. I first got the application form when I was fifteen, but I chickened out and didn't fill it in,' he later explained. 'I did the same thing the following year, but when I was seventeen and the form came through the door I was finally brave enough to fill it in.'

Before licking the stamp and trotting off to the post box, however, he first sought assurances from his sixth-form tutors that he could return to the college if he had second thoughts. And even then, as the day of the auditions loomed ever nearer he developed a nasty case of cold feet and might well have missed out on everything that has happened to him since had it not been for his mum forcing him to get dressed and pushing him out of the door with a kiss for good luck. 'I was really nervous,' he told the Bradford *Telegraph & Argus*. 'But she told me just to get on with it and not miss my chance.'

> **'It's weird to see how much you can fit into a year, like how much stuff you can do and how different your life can become.'**
> – Zayn

'In the end I decided to go along to Manchester just for the experience, and if I didn't make it, then I didn't,' he revealed in *One Direction: Forever Young*. 'When I got through the first stage and stood before the judges I thought I'd been kept [back] so they could take the mickey out of me.

'I was really shaky beforehand and when I got out on stage I was suddenly faced by all these people. I had to take a deep breath to calm myself. There were people as far as the eye could see! And Simon Cowell was sitting in front of me; it was amazing but terrifying at the same time. I know he doesn't exactly hold back with the criticism, so I was really worried about what he would say.'

For his audition in front of Simon, Zayn performed Mario's 2004 US Number One 'Let Me Love You', as he believed the ballad suited his voice. Yet, while Simon agreed with his choice of song – as indeed did Louis Walsh and Nicole Scherzinger – he also issued the caveat that Zayn needed to be 'hungrier for it' if he was going to progress in the competition. 'I think Simon gets you as a person from the minute he meets you,' Zayn reflected on his initial encounter with the man who was to change his life. 'I think he was right [because] at that point I didn't yet want it in the way I should have done, and he knew it. But the further I got into the competition the more and more I wanted it.'

Somewhat ironically, given that she was the driving force in getting Zayn to go to the audition, his mum has since struggled to get used to waving her son off. 'When he leaves home I cry at the gate and he says, "Mum! I'm not going to war!"' she recently told reporters. 'A driver comes for him and I have to stand there and wave back at him crying.'

42-year-old Tricia has also revealed that while Zayn may be thousands of miles from home, her dutiful son is never too busy to send his mum a text before bedtime. 'I don't

expect Zayn to text me all the time,' she said. 'But I text him, "Night night, son," and he texts back, "Love you, mum."'

As we know, Zayn is as fond of tweeting as he is texting, and his tweets informing his mum that he's coming home for a few days alert his legion of fans, who flock to the house and set up camp outside the gate. 'Fans ask me for permission to marry him,' she added. 'But he can choose his own Mrs.'

In the ITV documentary, *One Direction: A Year In The Making*, Zayn – having bemoaned getting up at three in the morning on the day of the auditions, revealed that all he'd wanted from the audition was a yes: 'I just wanted somebody to tell me I could sing.' In a separate interview he was rather more candid: 'When I auditioned for the show, I just did it for the experience. I think I was scared of being rejected, so when I kept getting through to the next stage it was just crazy. I thought they were only putting me through for a joke and that people were laughing at how bad I was.'

Though Zayn had given up the notion that he'd only been put through as a joke by the time he arrived at Bootcamp, he was still harbouring doubts about his ability. However, his confidence received something of a boost when Simon brought everyone together and told them that one of them was going to win the competition. Like everyone else in the room, Zayn was instantly struck with the thought, 'Oh my God, that could be me,' but on seeing the same twinkle in everyone else's eyes he crept back into his shell. For though he'd earned his right to be there, he automatically assumed they must be better than him and that he was simply making up the numbers. 'I like competition, but when I heard the other guys who were in my category I thought they were absolutely amazing,' he subsequently revealed. 'I don't have the highest voice in the world, so a Michael Jackson song ["Man In The Mirror"] wasn't the easiest for me to sing. I thought it was going to end for me there. I was preparing to go home every time there was a cut, and I knew how horrible it was going to feel. I was so happy when I got through that first day.'

While there was a far more relaxed mood in camp on the second day following Simon's announcement that there would be no cuts, Zayn was left feeling far from composed when he discovered that day's itinerary included learning a dance routine with Brian Friedman. 'I was absolutely horrified. I cannot dance to save my life,' Zayn revealed. 'A lot of people were from dancing backgrounds and had experience, but this was a totally new thing for me and I wasn't getting it at all. I found it so frustrating, and it made me feel like I didn't want to be there. I know that sounds bad, when I had this great opportunity, but I felt really self-conscious in front of everyone.'

> **'I think it's nice to have support from anyone out there, but for them to be female is always better!'**
> **– Zayn**

Rather than risk making a fool of himself in front of everyone as Brian put the hopefuls through their paces to Lady GaGa's 'Telephone', Zayn snuck backstage hoping that no one would notice. But of course, everyone did – including a very disgruntled Simon: 'Simon came to find me and he wasn't happy,' Zayn revealed. 'He told me I was wrong to bottle it, and he pointed out that if I didn't give it a go, I'd never be able to do it. He basically said that I should try it or I'd be messing things up for myself, which made sense.'

This was Simon's polite way of telling Zayn that if he didn't go out front, he might as well get his coat and go home. It was a no-brainer really, because while telling your friends and family that you didn't get through because you weren't good enough is one thing, telling them that you didn't get through because you were too embarrassed to dance in front of some guys you'd never met before is another matter entirely. Having been made to see the error of his ways by Simon, the two shook hands and Zayn put on his dancing shoes. This, of course, was a side of Simon that the public doesn't usually see, and when his local newspaper subsequently asked Zayn if television's resident 'Mr. Nasty' was as fearsome as he appears on *The X Factor*, Zayn laughingly replied: 'Simon's top. He's not frightening at all. He's just a big teddy bear.'

While Zayn may claim to be the 'shy one' in One Direction, he's also the token bad boy in the band as he's the only one who smokes – despite his ongoing New Year's resolutions to quit his habit. Aside from his nicotine addiction, he's also developed something of a fascination with inking up, and will surely be rivalling Rihanna in the tattoo stakes if he carries on. To date, aside from a Yin Yang symbol on his wrist, and a picture of crossed fingers on his forearm, he has his late grandfather's name, Walter, written in Arabic on his chest, a 'born lucky' symbol and a playing card on his stomach, and a silver fern on his neck. On his last two visits to the tattoo parlour he came away with 'Be true to who you are' in Arabic across his collarbone and, most recently, a microphone on his right forearm.

CHAPTER THREE

WHO'S THE DADDY

Liam James Payne

Place of Birth: Wolverhampton, West Midlands

Date of Birth: 29 August 1993

Star Sign: Virgo

'I had a really nice upbringing. I come from a typical
working-class background. My dad works in a factory, building
aeroplanes, and my mum is a nursery nurse. I was planning to go and
work in the factory with my dad, to do an apprenticeship,
but dad wasn't all that keen – he wanted me to sing!'

While most carefree eighteen-year-olds, whose offspring are as yet nothing more than a futuristic twinkle in their mind's eye, would undoubtedly shy away from being called 'Daddy' by their colleagues, Liam positively revels in being the sensible one in One Direction.

Like Louis and Zayn, Liam has only female siblings – Ruth and Nicola – both of whom are older than himself. And while he enjoys a close relationship with Ruth, as Nicola is the oldest of the three – and so was charged with the responsibility of looking after Liam and Ruth whenever their parents went out for the evening – Liam tended to look upon her more as a surrogate mother than as a big sister.

Of course, one reason why Nicola fussed and fretted over her little brother was because Liam – who was born some three weeks prematurely – was 'effectively born dead', as he himself phrased it, and for the first few years of his life seemed to be constantly ill. 'The doctors couldn't get a reaction from me, so I had to be brought round,' he explained in *Dare To Dream*. 'And although it seemed like I was okay, there were underlying problems.'

Indeed, there were. Yet despite being repeatedly taken into hospital by his anxious parents, Karen and Geoff, for what must have seemed like endless tests, the doctors didn't discover the source of the problem until Liam was four: one kidney wasn't functioning and was scarred. However, while the human body can function perfectly well with just the one kidney, Liam's problem was exacerbated because his other kidney was only functioning at 95 percent capacity. It got to the stage where he had to endure a mind-boggling 32 injections, morning and evening, each and every day to help his body cope with the strain and ease the pain. 'I've still got both kidneys, but one doesn't work,' he says today. 'I have to be careful not to drink too much, even water, and I have to keep myself as healthy as possible.'

One means of ensuring that he kept himself in shape was joining the school cross-country running team, which he did after inadvertently coming first in a race. However, while those closest to Liam were naturally thrilled at his success, his unexpected triumph left one particular nose out of joint. 'There was a guy who was running for Wolverhampton at the time and he was one of the best runners around, and I beat him, so everyone said that I'd cheated,' he explained. 'The next week we ran the same race and I won again, and that's how I found out that I could run.'

'My mates used to wind me up and pretend that girls liked me when they didn't. I'd then ask them out and they'd say no . . . which was mortifying.' – Liam

He didn't have much luck with any of the school's other sports teams, but having found a sport he excelled at, Liam decided to dedicate his life to running. He thought nothing of getting out of bed each morning at 6:00am – again, regardless of the weather – and going for a run before going off to school. Indeed, such was his dedication that, although he was only twelve years old, the PE teacher put him in with the school's under-eighteens team – a challenge he rose to with aplomb. He also joined the Wolverhampton and Bilston running team, and for three of the next five years he was the third best runner in his age group in the entire country. 'I used to get up and run five miles before school, and another few miles when I came home,' he subsequently revealed. 'At that time it was always a choice between running or singing, but I just missed out on a place in the England team. I didn't enjoy the running as much as my singing and that really made my mind up for me.'

Liam was also invited to join the school's basketball team, but once again he found that his talent for the sport – coupled with the snazzy basketball outfits he'd purchased whilst holidaying in America – didn't sit too well with some of the older kids, who resorted to bullying him. Rather than simply report these green-eyed oppressors to the teachers, his parents decided Liam should take boxing lessons so that he could stand up to his tormentors. 'It wasn't the nicest gym in the world, and you had to fight

everyone – regardless of age or size,' he recalled. 'So there I was, at twelve-years-old, fighting the 38-year-old trainer. I broke my nose, had a perforated eardrum, and I was always coming home with a bruised, puffy face. But it gave me so much confidence. It was nerve-wracking at first, but I got pretty good over the next couple of years.'

Of course, the school bullies were unaware of Liam's evening visits to the gym, but they soon found out, as he explains: 'They chased me into the road [and] it all got too much so I stood up to them and ended up having a fight with one of them. Thankfully, I won, but I nearly got kicked out of school for it, which obviously wasn't ideal.'

Aside from running and squaring up to bullies, Liam was 'always busy doing singing gigs, that's how I used to make my money'. While the gigs in question involved nothing more than getting up and belting out the latest chart hits on a karaoke machine, aside from putting a few quid in his piggy bank, it undoubtedly put him in good stead for the future. 'I was always singing karaoke when I was growing up,' he said. 'I used to get up anywhere and sing Robbie Williams songs. I did my first rendition of "Let Me Entertain You" at a holiday camp when I was about six, and I didn't stop from then on. I also used to put my dad's glasses on, clasp my hands behind my back and sing along to Oasis CDs, pretending to be Liam Gallagher.'

Needless to say, his dad's sunglasses remained at home when he was selected for one of the solos when his school choir participated in an all-school choral ensemble which set a world record for singing the same song – Bill Withers's 1972 US Number One 'Lean On Me' – in unison.

When he was thirteen, Liam followed in his sisters' footsteps by signing up with a local performing arts group, Pink Productions. But while he would later boast about how much he'd enjoyed the dance routines at Bootcamp, back then he literally had to

be pushed out onto the stage, as his teacher Jodie Richards revealed to the Wolverhampton *Express & Star*: 'He was really timid when he first started,' she said. 'He wanted to sing after watching his sisters, so he joined us by taking a singing-only role in his first show, but I literally had to push him onto the stage he was so petrified. Who would have thought it when you see him on *X Factor* today?'

However, after receiving encouragement from the girls in the group, Liam decided to do the next show as a full cast member, and he never looked back. 'It was clear very early on that Liam had something special and that he had a natural talent,' Jodie explained. 'He's stayed with us right up until the latest *X Factor* auditions, taking part in three or four shows a year. I speak to him every day on the phone and told him we want him back for the Christmas production. His sisters are really proud of him although they are upset at the thought that this could mean him leaving. They're a really close family.'

Jodie and Liam's fellow performers at Pink Productions were naturally just as supportive when he tried out for *The X Factor* in 2008. 'We told him to do it for the experience as he was only fourteen, and he ended up at Simon Cowell's house in Barbados, only just failing to go through to the live shows,' 27-year-old Jodie revealed. 'But he was told to try again and he's spent the last two years working towards that, getting experience and building up a fan base. I've taken him on regional tours, singing in clubs and festivals and I think that's given him the confidence to perform in front of anyone.

'He's a lovely lad with a strong sense of who he is. He's not big-headed at all. He's struggled in some roles but he's not a diva, he would never refuse to do a part. He works hard and he always has. He's even won a few of our personality trophies through being such a character.'

According to Jodie, Liam's winning ways with the girls played no small part in inspiring some top performances from female students, who were all eager to join his senior group. And needless to say, Jodie believes the routines Liam has learnt during his time at Pink Productions, in a wide range of musicals from camp rock to action

> 'I was always singing karaoke when I was growing up. I used to get up anywhere and sing Robbie Williams songs.'
> – Liam

movie and boogie and punk, stood him in good stead for *The X Factor*. 'In my six and a half years running the classes, I must have trained at least 400 pupils and he's the one who deserves it the most,' she said. 'He said he wanted to be famous and enjoy his life, and I really believe this time he'll do it.'

Like the rest of the boys, Liam went through the usual experiments with his style, and knows the photographic evidence is lurking somewhere at the back of his parents' cupboards. 'Judging by the photographs of me growing up, my hair has kind of come full circle. I had a big mushroom when I was a kid, then I had tramlines put in the side of my head,' he revealed. 'After that, I shaved it all off to grade three, then grew it long again, so it's now similar to how it was when I was a kid. Despite my hair mistakes, I think I got away with it at school. I had a girlfriend called Charnelle in Reception, who used to send me love letters. I was also really proud of the fact that I went out with a girl who was in Year Six when I was in Year Four. She was one of my sister's friends, and I thought I was really cool having an older girlfriend.'

While Zayn and Harry seem to get all the attention in the media for being lady-killers, Liam is something of a dark horse when it comes to the girls. By his own admission, he's always preferred female company and would much rather have them as girlfriends rather than just friends. Nor was he afraid of wooing the object of his desires with a song to get their attention, but going around crooning the love songs of the day didn't always work out as planned: 'I really liked one girl called Emily and asked her out 22 times, but she always said no,' he revealed. 'Finally I sang to her and she said she'd go out with me, but she dumped me the next day.'

Of course, being an old-fashioned romantic wasn't without its pitfalls, as he explained in *Dare To Dream*. 'My mates used to wind me up and pretend that girls liked me when they didn't. I'd [then] ask them out and they'd say no . . . which was mortifying.'

Though he was in a steady relationship when he entered the 2010 series of *The X Factor*,

'The only thing I really wanted to do was see Simon Cowell and I waited
nine hours in a queue to get that chance, but it was definitely worth it.'

– Liam

the attendant pressures of his being away from home for extended periods proved too much to bear. However, as with every dark cloud, Liam's silver lining came in the form of one of the show's dancers, Danielle Peazer, and they've been seeing each other ever since.

However, Danielle – who also works as a backing dancer for The Saturdays and Jessie J – has been subjected to moronic death threats on Twitter because of her relationship with Liam. 'I think it's horrible how people can [do] such nasty things and not even think of how it affects people,' Liam said in a candid interview with *Now* magazine, in which he not only spoke openly about their relationship, but also hinted that Danielle may well be the one. 'Danielle's amazing,' he went on. 'All the boys love her – in a friendly way. Lately I've been able to spend a lot of time with her. It's hard when we go away, but she's so good about everything.'

When asked in a separate interview with the *Teen Now* how he might have reacted had the rest of the boys not liked Danielle, he said: 'No, it wouldn't bother me if I really liked her. I'd listen to what they had to say and make my own mind up. But also there would be no one else after my girlfriend, so that's good!'

Unlike Zayn, Liam – though he was only fourteen at the time – readily filled out his application form for the 2008 *X Factor* series and popped it in the post. For though his running prowess was deemed good enough to see him placed on the reserve list for the 2012 Olympics, he'd lost the thrill of the chase and desperately wanted to prove that he had other strings to his bow. And while his mates were obviously all aware of his singing skills – if only from watching him warbling to various girls in the playground – hearing that he'd applied to go on national television still came as something of an eye-opener. 'When I told my mates I was going in for *The X Factor* we had a bit of banter because they thought it was quite funny, but they were also supportive,' he said.

Though supportive, his friends would have undoubtedly given him a further ribbing had they been aware of his main reason for going on the show, as he himself subsequently revealed: 'The only thing I really wanted to do was see Simon Cowell and I waited nine hours in a queue to get that chance, but it was definitely worth it.

'I felt quite grown-up at the time, and like I was capable of handling everything that came with being on the show. But looking back now at all we've been through, there is no way I could have handled it – no way at all. If I had made the live shows I wouldn't have known what hit me,' he explained. 'JLS and Alexandra Burke were in that year and I would have been gone straight away.' Liam is doing himself something of a disservice here, because he effortlessly sailed through the audition stages.

A lucky escape, of course, occurred at Bootcamp, where he came within a whisper of being sent home when it appeared that Simon, Louis, Cheryl and Dannii were going to put Rikki Loney through in his stead. But as Rikki – who would, of course, make it through to the live finals the following year – stood out on stage waiting to learn his fate, Simon suddenly decided that they'd made the wrong choice and convinced Louis and the girls to keep Liam. 'I was convinced it was over,' a bemused, but no less ecstatic Liam told the *Wolverhampton Express & Star* upon his return home. 'But then a woman came out and said the judges wanted to see me again. It was only later I found out about Rikki.'

Having been granted what must have seemed like an eleventh-hour stay of execution,

Liam, together with his mum Karen, who was serving as his appointed chaperone, was flown out to Simon's home in Barbados. Sadly, however, Liam being chosen over Rikki would prove to be the extent of Simon's patronage as he was rejected at the Judges' Houses stage, as Simon considered him to be unprepared for the rigours of the live show finals. '[I] sang Take That's "A Million Love Songs", but Simon didn't take me through, because he didn't think I was ready for it,' he explained in *One Direction: Forever Young*. 'He said to me at the time, "You need to go and get your GCSEs," so that's what I did.'

While revealing that it had been 'horrible' to get rejected at the Judges' Houses stage, Liam was gracious enough to recognise his limitations at that time. Of course, little could he have known that the heartache of rejection would turn out to be a blessing in disguise.

Liam said that, while he followed Simon's advice by going back to St Peter's Collegiate School to concentrate on his GCSEs, having to return to normality after having his dreams crushed at such a pivotal stage on *The X Factor* wasn't without its drawbacks. 'It was tough to go back to school afterwards, though, having been on TV in front of sixteen million people,' he explained. 'All of a sudden you're in a Spanish lesson you don't want to be in, so it's a bit of a comedown. Not that I ever got bullied because of the show. I was just always the boy who had been on *The X Factor*, so if anything it was cool.'

'It's strange going from being totally unknown to being on the front of magazines and winning polls and things like that.'
— Liam

One thing he did upon his return to Wolverhampton was to take a couple of his school pals to see JLS when *The X Factor*'s eventual runners-up played the Oceana, as well as meet up with the boys at their hotel. One of the lucky pair was Michael Coates, who'd been in the choir with Liam, and had also entered a school talent contest with him in Year Nine when they'd performed R. Kelly's 1999 hit 'If I Could Turn Back The Hands Of Time'. 'We went to their hotel, the Britannia. Liam told them we used to sing together and he got me to sing the R. Kelly song. I couldn't believe I was singing to JLS.'

As Liam spent his every waking moment dreaming of becoming a pop star, it was perhaps inevitable that his school work began to suffer. Thankfully for him, his head of year had been monitoring the situation and provided the wake-up call Liam needed by asking him what he might do if he left school without any recognisable qualifications, and his voice breaking further down the line meant that he couldn't sing anymore? 'That really hit me, and I started working a lot harder from then on,' he revealed about his 'cruel to be kind' encounter. 'I ended up getting one A* in PE as well as two Bs, six Cs and a D. The school wanted me to carry on and do A-levels, but I went to music college instead.'

Liam's parents were no doubt thrilled at his acquiring an A* in PE, as they'd already mooted the idea of his taking up a career as a PE teacher. However, while both are obviously thrilled that he is finally following his dream, they are still struggling to come to terms with the fact that their son is now an international superstar. 'I'm incredibly proud

of Liam and think of the other boys as our extended family,' Karen said in an interview with the *Wolverhampton Express & Star*. 'I was in HMV the other day and saw Liam and the boys on all the posters, CD covers and calendars. I had this huge grin on my face, thinking, "That's my son." You have to pinch yourself because it doesn't feel real.'

While he'd accrued more than enough qualifications to land a decent-paying job out in the nine-to-five world, Liam still harboured dreams of making it as a pop star, and performed at several high-profile events in and around Wolverhampton, such as the Party in the Park in Stourbridge (with Rikki Loney also on the bill). He appeared with Same Difference when the 2007 *X Factor* finalists performed at Molineux Stadium, the home of Wolverhampton Wanderers, during the half-time break when Wolves were entertaining Manchester United, and he also supported Peter Andre.

The money he earned went towards singing lessons and setting up his own website, where fans could buy signed photos and other merchandise. It also paid for the services of various producers and writers who helped him to hone his talents. He was, however, careful not to sign with anyone for fear of scuppering his chances of being accepted on *The X Factor* at a later date.

In spite of his thorough preparation for the 2010 *X Factor*, Liam later admitted to feeling nervous second time around, simply because he wanted the chance to show Simon how much he'd improved. 'To me, that second audition was my chance to prove to Simon that I've got what it takes,' he revealed. 'I went there with one aim – to get a yes from him. Of course, it also mattered to me what the other judges thought, but I guess because I had history with him I wanted to know that he felt I'd improved and moved on and grown up since he'd last seen me.' Liam also said that, while he was willing to take the risk of being rejected a second time, there were those amongst his family and friends who were worried for him. 'Some people advised me against it – I think because they were worried that I'd get hurt,' he said. 'But most people were really supportive, which meant the world to me.'

This time round Liam took to the stage at Birmingham's LG Arena with far more confidence and Simon was quick to recognise that his voice had also improved in that time. So much so, in fact, that his heartfelt rendition of the classic jazz ballad 'Cry Me A River' – later covered by Michael Bublé – earned him a standing ovation from Simon and guest judge Natalie Imbruglia, who thought his performance 'really impressive.' 'I think other people in this competition should be a little bit worried about you. You're really good,' she told him, while Cheryl Cole declared: 'You've definitely got it, whatever it is, you have got it.' Having eulogised Liam, Louis Walsh then turned on Simon for failing to put Liam through to the live shows first time around. But Simon remained unfazed: 'He wasn't quite ready when he came to my house two years ago,' he shrugged. 'I said to him then come back in two years time and you are going to be a different person. I got it right.'

'This show has already changed my life because if I hadn't come on the show I would be working in a factory.'
– Liam

When asked for a comment on making it through to the Bootcamp stage for a second time by his local newspaper, the *Wolverhampton Express & Star*, a thrilled Liam said: 'This show has already changed my life because if I hadn't come on the show I would be working in a factory.'

While Liam arrived in London knowing what would be expected of him at Bootcamp, one unexpected twist came with his sharing a hotel room with his future bandmate Niall. 'We got on really well. We had a laugh and sang songs together,' he revealed. 'We were practicing a lot too, but there were long days with a lot of work, so when we got back to the hotel, most of the time we just wanted to chill out and have a laugh.'

Liam certainly wasn't laughing when it came time for him to perform in front of the judges. 'Having such a good first audition is a brilliant bonus, but it's also a negative thing getting great comments, because it meant that I felt like I had so much to live up to,' he explained. 'I'd messed things up a bit in rehearsals, which put me even more on edge because in that situation there's no such thing as starting again. There was only one thing on my mind, and that was to prove to Simon that I meant business and show that I had what it takes. As soon as I got on stage I told the judges, "The reason why I think I've got the 'X' factor is because I had a knock-back at an early age, I took on a huge challenge, I set myself a huge goal and I never gave up." Then I went for it.'

Unfortunately for Liam, another knock-back was waiting as Simon, Louis, and Nicole deemed his performance of Oasis' 2002 Number Two single 'Stop Crying Your Heart Out' as inadequate. 'Finding out I hadn't made it to Judges' Houses was crushing,' he revealed. 'I honestly thought that was the end of everything and I was so upset.'

Of course, as we all know now, Liam wasn't left crying his heart out for very long . . .

CHAPTER FOUR

PLUCK OF THE IRISH

Niall James Horan

Place of Birth: Mullingar, County Westmeath, Ireland

Date of Birth: 13 September 1993

Star Sign: Virgo

'The town where I live is quite small and there isn't much for young people to do. I spent most of my time just hanging out with my friends or singing, and obviously all that singing is what led me to *The X Factor*. When I went along for the audition I was a student and had just finished my GCSEs. I was planning to go to university and study Civil Engineering, which would have been a bit different from the pop-star route.'

Niall is something of an odd one out in One Direction. Not only is he the only member of the band to have a brother, as well as no female siblings, he's also the only blond in the line-up, and the only one who can speak a foreign language (Spanish). And on top of that, he's the only one who received his pocket money in Euros, as he hails from the sleepy market town of Mullingar, in the Republic of Ireland.

Following the breakdown of his parents' marriage when he was five, Niall and his older brother Greg first lived with their mother, Maura, in nearby Edgeworthstown, and then flitted between their parents' respective houses before eventually settling in with dad, Bobby, in Mullingar. 'I ended up moving in with my dad because he lived in town, so I had more friends there and it was more convenient for school and other stuff,' Niall explained.

With all the emotional turmoil that accompanies a family upheaval such as divorce, one might have expected the two brothers to become closer, but nothing could be further from the truth, as Niall explains: 'We hated each other when we were growing up. I think of him in those days as the annoying older brother [while] he thinks I was the annoying younger brother. I hated it whenever he even looked at me [and] I used to try and be the big man and hang around with all of his mates, and he hated that. We used to fight all the time, which wasn't great as he was a lot older and bigger than me.'

The sibling rivalry continued until Greg had left school – by which time Niall was thirteen or so – and the two started to get along, eventually settling their differences and becoming best friends. Indeed, their relationship was such that, when stories began to spread about supposed feuding between the boys over Harry and Liam hogging the limelight as *The X Factor*'s competition heated up, 23-year-old Greg stepped in to rubbish the rumours: 'It's absolute nonsense. The boys all get on really well together. They instantly bonded and have become the best of friends,' he told the *Irish Herald*. 'They have a huge amount of respect for each other. They have gelled so well that it's like they have already known each other for ten years.

'I loved school. I liked it all the way through right up until I left – apart from having to do the homework, which I hated.'
– Niall

'I'm so proud of Niall,' he continued. 'He is getting on great. He rang a few times during the week but I don't want to talk to him because I just miss him so much. He is loving every second of the experience, and the lads are all fantastic. I've met them all twice now and I'm flying over again.'

Niall was a keen singer from an early age, and Arthur Fallon, the principal of his primary school, St. Kenny National, told the *Herald* that he remembered Niall's lead role in a school play in 2004 when he was just nine years old. 'He had the lead part in "Oliver" in 2004, he was in fourth class. I remember that song "Where Is Love", he sang that song, it's a very difficult song, and he sang it and it was very moving.'

Like Liam, Niall was somewhat small for his age. But whereas Liam was forced to fight fire with fire, Niall's happy-go-lucky attitude, and his 'always being up for having a laugh and messing around' appealed to all his playground peers. Indeed, how he came to befriend his best mate is worthy of a mention in itself. 'I remember a Geography lesson on my first day at secondary school [Colaiste Mhuire]. All my friends [from St Kenny National School] had been put in a different class so I felt like I was back to square one and I didn't know anyone,' he explained. 'Then the guy behind me, Nicky, farted and I started laughing, and we became friends. From then on we were like best mates.'

Niall then went on to describe how he and his flatulent friend would sit at the back of the class either harmonising on traditional Irish songs or thinking up ways – other than farting – to make each other laugh. 'The teachers used to be raging with us. I never got into serious trouble, though, apart from the one time when we bunked off school for the day and I got caught. We all got properly told off for that.'

'I loved school,' he subsequently reflected. 'I liked it all the way through right up until I left – apart from having to do the homework, which I hated, and general studying, which I didn't do much of. Although I wasn't necessarily academic, I think I was intelligent, but the simple fact is that I spent too much time messing around. I thought school was all about having the "Craic" and acting like a fool.'

St. Kenny's deputy principle, Ann Caulfield, remembers things rather differently, and told the *Irish Herald*: 'He is remembered for his manners and his personality as much as his singing. He was a little saintly child in the classroom and every other teacher would say the same. A very, very, good boy.' While Niall's French teacher, Georgina Ainscough (his favourite teacher), said, 'He genuinely is a lovely boy and he really deserves to do well.'

'I did okay in terms of grades all the way through school, and my teachers were always saying I had lots of potential,' Niall said. 'But I was too busy messing around or playing football with my mates to really get down to work. One of my teachers told my mum that I was always in a world of my own when I was in class.'

It would seem Niall was also in something of a world of his own when it came to setting hairstyle trends during his formative years, as he sheepishly recalled: 'When I was about eleven or twelve I got a "V" shaved into the back of my head and left it longer on the sides. I was looking at photos when I went home recently and I have to say it looked disgusting on me. I think everyone has those embarrassing photos of mistakes they made when they were young, but some of mine were particularly bad.'

Strutting about town with a 'V' shaved into the back of one's neck arguably isn't

'I started playing guitar when I was about twelve and a year later I went in for a school talent contest.'
– Niall

the best way of attracting the opposite sex, but Niall says that at that particular time having a girlfriend didn't feature too high on his list of priorities. 'I never really had any girlfriends in the early days at school because I didn't see the point in being tied down at ten or whatever,' he said. 'I was always shy about that kind of thing in any case. I had my first kiss when I was eleven, but I think I've blocked it out of my mind because it was so bad. [In fact] I'm not sure it even counts as a kiss. I had a girlfriend when I was about thirteen, but we didn't stay together for very long, and I've not really been out with many people since.'

At the time of making that particular disclosure Niall was insisting that he'd 'still never had a serious girlfriend', but since his becoming one of the pop world's most eligible bachelors his name has been linked with several beauties, including the American singer and actress Demi Lovato, who set the glossies gossiping by revealing she had a crush on Niall, as well as calling him 'adorable' in an interview with MSN UK. Niall, of course, has made no secret of his thoughts about Demi, who enjoyed a US Number One album in 2009 with *Here We Go Again*. And while his adoring female fans wouldn't be overly pleased to see him taken off the market, Niall's mum Maura told the *Irish Herald* that Demi would have her 'blessing'. Having said that, however, she was careful to add that she'd 'never turn any girl of Niall's away, that's the kind of mother I am'.

'I never really had any girlfriends in the early days at school because I didn't see the point in being tied down at ten or whatever.'
– Niall

And when asked about her son's success the beaming Maura added: 'It makes me very emotional seeing what he's doing, it really is changing his life – it's so huge. What else could a mother ask for her child? It's mind blowing. Niall's was the only name I have heard being chanted in America, it was especially nice because for me, it was great to hear that. He's a great head on his shoulders [and] he's very humble. I always warn him to be nice to the girls and always chat to them and pose for pictures.'

Perhaps not surprisingly, the one lesson in which Niall always paid attention at Colaiste Mhuire was music, and having started out playing the recorder and singing in the school choir, he soon graduated to rock'n'roll guitar. 'I started playing when I was about twelve and a year later I went in for a school talent contest,' he said.

His performance of The Script's 'The Man Who Can't Be Moved', which appeared on the Dublin-based band's eponymous 2008 debut album, and scored a Number Two hit on the UK chart when it was released as a single in July 2008, won Niall his first press coverage. 'My mate Kieron accompanied me on guitar, and although it wasn't a competition or anything, I got really good coverage in the local paper because they had someone at the show taking photos.'

Rather than rest on his laurels, Niall – with best friend, Kieron again providing the accompaniment – entered a local talent competition in which he sang Chris Brown's 'With You', which gave Brown a Number Two on the *Billboard* singles chart following its release in 2007. 'I won the show, which was amazing,' a proud Niall recalled of his first taste of success while performing in the competitive arena. 'It made me think that maybe singing was something I was okay at.'

Following on from there, Niall had his first brush with the TV show that was to change his life when he supported 2009 *X Factor* finalist, Lloyd Daniels, at a local music venue called the Academy. 'I told him [Daniels] I was going for it [*The X Factor*] too, but he didn't seem that convinced about it,' Niall recalled. 'Later, he came to one of the live shows and I bumped into him. He remembered me and said, "See, I told you to go for it." But he actually didn't.'

In November 2009, Niall also participated in a local 'Stars In Their Eyes' talent show, in which he sang Jason Mraz's 2008 Grammy-nominated hit, 'I'm Yours'. 'I had a great time,' he recalled. 'I did really well and got some good press again. And it was all useful practice for the future.'

Someone who had always known he would 'go for it' once he was old enough was his auntie, who came over from America every summer to holiday with the rest of the Horan family in Galway, on Ireland's west coast. 'Once when we were driving along I was singing in the back of the car and she thought the radio was on,' he said. 'Exactly the same thing happened to Michael Bublé with his dad. He's an absolute hero, so I like the fact that we have a similar story. My auntie said she always knew I'd be famous from then on, and she said it the entire time I was growing up.'

'When I was in Dublin, I looked around and there was like eight thousand people at the auditions and I'm thinking, "Not a hope."' – Niall

While Niall's mum had always believed her youngest would make a name for himself as a solo artist, she knew that he would be equally committed to making One Direction a success: 'One thing I do know,' she told the *Westmeath Examiner*, 'is that he is completely committed and focused on his singing. He'd sing for his breakfast, dinner and supper.'

Niall had always known that he wanted to give *The X Factor* a go, but when he applied for the 2010 series he wasn't holding out much hope of being taken up. 'I looked around, and there was like 8000 people at the auditions and I'm thinking, "Not a hope,"' he confessed in *One Direction: A Year In The Making*. Indeed, when the Dublin auditions were held at the city's Convention Centre on 28 June, he'd just started his Leaving Certificate. 'The plan was to go to university and study sound engineering, but obviously that all changed once I got through to the live finals,' he said. 'At that point everything got put on hold, but not surprisingly, I didn't mind a bit.'

However, his dream to be recognised as an artist and respected for his music was almost shattered when his rendition of Ne-Yo's 2006 transatlantic hit 'So Sick' failed to make much of an impression on the judges. Louis was in favour of putting him through,

'Simon told me I'd chosen the wrong song and that I wasn't prepared enough. But he still said he liked me, which was a massive bonus.'
– Niall

while Cheryl voted against. Though guest judge Katy Perry, who was standing in for Dannii, shared Cheryl's reservations about Niall's ability, she knew from experience what it was like to get a break and gave him the nod, which meant his fate lay in Simon's hands.

After much deliberation, Simon decided to go with his gut instinct and put him through to the Bootcamp stage – but only after issuing the well-worn *X Factor* caveat that his performance would have to improve dramatically if he wanted to advance further in the competition. 'Simon told me I'd chosen the wrong song and [that] I wasn't prepared enough. But he still said he liked me, which was a massive bonus,' Niall said in *One Direction: Forever Young*. 'Cheryl said no, but in the end I got three "yes" votes because Louis [Walsh] more or less forced one out of Katy [Perry]. That was enough to put me through to Bootcamp. Of course, I would have loved the full four, but as long as I was going to the next round I didn't mind too much.'

As previously mentioned, Niall found himself sharing a hotel room with Liam. 'It was a real laugh staying at the hotel, but it got totally wrecked one night. It wasn't us though, honestly,' he later revealed. 'I was fast asleep at the time it was happening. I remember someone kicking the door of my room at about two o'clock in the morning and it woke me up. And then the next morning when I left, there was broken glass and mess everywhere. I know who was responsible, but I'm not telling.'

> 'That's the worst thing I've ever had happen to me in my life. I was standing there waiting for my name to be called out, and then I wasn't. I was so upset.'
> – Niall

While he and Liam got on great and 'had the Craic', as Niall is fond of saying, he also admits to finding the first day of Bootcamp a rather more sobering experience. 'Louis [Walsh] said they were looking for a star, and they were only going to pick the best people,' he revealed. 'Half of all the contestants were being sent home on that first day, so it was pretty scary. By the end of that very day it could have all been over for me, and I could have been getting on a plane back to Ireland. Before we left for the day, we were given a list of 40 songs and we had to pick one to perform the next day, then go away and practice it. Louis warned us that this could be our last chance and not to mess it up. No pressure then! I chose "Champagne Supernova" because I'm a big Oasis fan and I thought no one else would sing it. I was right as well – I was the only one at Bootcamp who chose the song.'

Sadly, while he was the only one to chose 'Champagne Supernova', there was to be no champagne celebration for Niall. 'That's the worst thing I've ever had happen to me in my life,' Niall reflected. 'I was standing there waiting for my name to be called out, and then I wasn't. I was so upset. I was so stupid that, even though we were five young lads standing together in a group, it never occurred to me that they might be thinking of putting us together in a band. Harry and I [had been] sitting outside with our suitcases ready to go home when they came and got us. We were sitting on the concourse of Wembley Arena feeling miserable and thinking it was all over.'

But of course, he was to be one of the lucky five asked to return and step up to the microphone.

CHAPTER FIVE

WILD ABOUT HARRY

Harry Edward Styles

Place of Birth: Evesham, Worcestershire
Date of Birth: 1 February 1994
Star Sign: Aquarius

'All I ever wanted was to do something that was well paid.
I could never really pinpoint what that would be, though. I really liked
the idea of being a singer, but I had no idea how to go about it.'

If Liam is the 'Daddy', Louis the 'Joker', Zayn the 'Pin-up' and Niall the 'Loveable Rogue', then cherubic Harry has to be the 'Face' of One Direction. For while those who have no interest in the pop charts would probably struggle to pick the others out of a line-up, with Harry's love life taking up as many column inches as his day job he's currently got one of the most readily identifiable faces in the country – if not the world. And while he's always been the apple of his doting mother Anne's eye, it would seem that the rest of the female population are also unable to take their eyes away from the angelic face that has launched a thousand quips.

Though he was born in Evesham, Worcestershire, the family moved to Holmes Chapel in Cheshire when he was four. When Harry and the rest of the boys paid a visit to his mum in the run-up to the 2010 *X Factor* final, the normally sedate leafy village became a hotbed of activity as hundreds of teenage girls gathered en masse outside Anne's home on London Road to catch a glimpse of Harry and the other boys.

Harry was left bewildered by the reception: 'I can't believe the number of people

'I always used to love singing. The first song I knew all the words to was "Girl Of My Best Friend" by Elvis.'
– Harry

outside. It's amazing,' he told the local newspaper, the *Crewe Chronicle*. 'It's brilliant to be home because this time next week we could potentially have won the show.' Asked if he had a message for the people of Holmes Chapel who had adorned the village with banners, balloons and signs saying 'Welcome Home Harry', he added: 'Everyone's been brilliant. It's a weird and wonderful feeling to have your home town all rooting for you.'

While the children at the local primary school, which Harry had himself attended, would have been equally thrilled to welcome their home-grown hero, they would undoubtedly have been interested to hear all about his first appearances under the spotlight in the school's somewhat unusual plays. 'I once played Buzz Lightyear in *Chitty Chitty Bang Bang*,' he subsequently explained. 'I know that sounds a bit weird, but basically when the children hid from the Child Catcher in the toy store they had Buzz and Woody in there, so I got to dress up as Buzz.'

Aside from going to 'infinity and beyond', Harry also apparently sneaked into his sister's bedroom and borrowed a pair of her grey tights to help him get into character for the lead role in another school play, as he later revealed: 'I played "Barney" [about a mouse that lived in a church] and I had to wear [the] tights and a headband with ears on and sing in front of everyone. I like to think I was a good mouse.'

'I've made a few style mistakes in my time. The worst thing was probably when I had blond streaks put in my hair when I was eight.'
– Harry

Sadly for Harry, wearing his sister's tights and sporting a Barney headband wouldn't be his only sartorial misfires during his early years: 'I've made a few style mistakes in my time,' he ruefully admits. 'The worst thing was probably when I had blond streaks put in [my hair] when I was eight. I looked a real chav. I thought it was cool when I went to school the day after having it done, but looking back I looked a douche.'

When he wasn't slapping on the greasepaint on stage, Harry liked nothing better than to sing along to his dad's record collection. 'I always used to love singing,' he explained. 'The first song I knew all the words to was "Girl Of My Best Friend" by Elvis. My dad introduced me to his music, and when I got given a karaoke machine by my granddad, my cousin and I recorded a load of Elvis tracks. I wish I still had them so I could have a listen.'

Like Niall, Harry admits to becoming easily distracted in the classroom as he grew older, which often resulted in his grades slipping below the standards his parents had come to expect. Having initially excelled in maths until he found things weren't quite adding up, he later took an interest in English – especially after the teacher complimented him on the quality of his writing – and was understandably proud when he scored an A for his first ever essay. But chatting to his mates or day-dreaming the lessons away, instead of thinking about ways to improve his writing, inevitably put paid to any ambitions he might have had of making a living from his storytelling.

'I worked pretty hard at school, but I enjoyed myself as well. Life is all about balance.' – Harry

Despite admitting to being easily distracted in the classroom, Harry says he has nothing but fond memories from his time at secondary school, Holmes Chapel Comprehensive: 'I worked pretty hard [at school], but I enjoyed myself as well. Life is all about balance,' he sagely reflected. 'I played badminton a lot. I liked the fact that it wasn't the most obvious sport to get into, and that you need quite a lot of skill to play it. My dad [Des] is really good at it, so I got that from him.

Aside from shuttling his cock over the net on the badminton court, Harry was equally keen on slamming a ball into the net on the football pitch – as much for the camaraderie as for the sport itself, as he explains: 'When I started playing for the local team in goal I made friends from other schools as well, which meant I had a lot of mates. I've always liked being around people and getting to know new people, so I've always had a wide group of friends.'

However, the affable Harry didn't restrict his ever-widening circle of friends to boys. 'I used to be friends with girls as well as boys,' he continues. 'I wasn't one of those boys who thought girls were smelly and didn't like them; I was kind of friends with everyone. I had a few girlfriends here and there when I was really young, but I didn't have an actual girlfriend until I was twelve. Then I went out with a girl called Emilie, and for quite a long time considering how young we were. I was also with a girl called Abi – I guess you could say that she was my first serious girlfriend.'

Harry, of course, was never going to struggle finding a girlfriend, regardless of what career path he chose, but it was only after he found fame on *The X Factor* that the girls

of Holmes Chapel gained an insight into his preferences. 'I don't have a type because with some girls I may not find them attractive immediately, but then I really get to like them because their personality is so attractive,' he revealed. 'I like someone I can have a conversation with, and I would always look for someone who could get on with my parents. It's important to me that my family like her too.'

This particular obviously also applied to his extended family, as when *Teen Now* magazine asked if he'd be put off if the other boys didn't like his new girlfriend, he responded: 'It would be nice if they approved. But if I liked her then I'd have to think about it. It is a big swaying point, 'cause if they liked her, it would probably make me like her a bit more.'

As was the case with Louis and Niall, Harry's world was turned upside down when his parents broke the news to him that they were splitting up. 'I'm such a mummy's boy, I'm really close to my dad as well . . . I think we're probably quite alike in a lot of ways.' He was only seven at the time, and while he admits to crying on discovering his life was about to change irrevocably, he said he quickly accepted the situation. 'I guess I didn't really get what was going on properly,' he's since explained. 'I was just sad that my parents wouldn't be together anymore.'

Following his parents' separation, Harry and Gemma flitted between his mum and dad's places for a while before moving away from Holmes Chapel altogether when his mum Anne took over a pub out in the Cheshire countryside, where they were to live for the next five years. And while subsequently admitting that – like Niall – he hadn't always seen eye to eye with his elder sibling, he says that he and Gemma have grown closer as they've gotten older.

During an interview with *Mizz* magazine in April 2011, Gemma revealed how she first came to recognise that her baby brother was destined for greater things: 'I've always been proud of my brother – he's almost annoyingly gifted . . . at everything. Any sport, any activity he tried, he'd be better than average – and look at that hair! So I'm glad that in the past year he's been given a chance to show off his talent.'

Though they've grown closer, Harry's fame has inevitably got in the way of their relationship, as Gemma explained: 'With all the attention comes a lot of hard work, which means we get to spend less time together [and] try fitting in Skype calls around a hectic schedule and the occasional eight-hour time difference!'

While relocating to a pub out in the sticks didn't involve passports or the crossing of borders, being taken away from everything he knew would still have been something of a culture shock for Harry – as, indeed, it probably was for his mum and Gemma. Thankfully, however, his enforced isolation was alleviated somewhat when he befriended an older kid called Reg, who was apparently the only other boy in the area.

> **'I used to be friends with girls as well as boys. I wasn't one of those boys who thought girls were smelly and didn't like them.'**
> **– Harry**

Additional recompense for all the upheaval came with Harry's discovery that there was an ice cream farm situated nearby. 'That first summer Reg and I used to go every day to [the] Great Budworth Ice Cream Farm, which was about two miles away,' he recalled. 'We'd borrow £2 off our mums and cycle up there and get an ice cream. I can remember that so clearly.' Such was his appreciation of the farm's iced delicacies that he's since taken the rest of the One Direction boys there to see – or rather taste – for themselves.

In 2006, Anne, Harry and Gemma returned to Holmes Chapel, and Harry hadn't been long reacquainting himself with the familiar landmarks when his mum met a local called Robin Twist, who was to become his stepdad. 'I really liked him [Robin] and I was always asking [mum] if he was coming over, but she wanted to make sure that Gemma and I were okay with him being around,' he later explained. 'She worried a lot, so in the end I used to text him and tell him to come over. I was really pleased when Robin proposed to mum. He did it completely by surprise while they were watching *Coronation Street* on Christmas Eve. I was at Abi's house at the time and I remember getting a call from my mum and how happy I was when she told me they were going to be getting married.'

As with Louis, Harry was surprised to be asked to try out as singer in a school band. Until he was approached by his friends, he had restricted his singing to either the shower or the car. And ambitious as it must have seemed, the would-be band harboured hopes of winning their school's rapidly approaching 'Battle of the Bands' competition, which was to be staged in the school canteen. 'I knew I could hold a note, but I had no idea how I'd be,' Harry later confessed. 'I'd always imagined what it would be like to be in a band, so I started practicing with them.'

Though all the musicians in the band were relative novices themselves, the quartet duly set about learning the chords and changes to Bryan Adams's 1985 classic, 'Summer Of '69', and Aussie rockers Jet's rather more recent 2003 hit, 'Are You Gonna Be My Girl'. 'We were all ready to go and we started filling out the application form, but we didn't have a name and we couldn't think of anything,' he said. 'It got to the day before the show and we had to put something down, so we decided just to go for something completely random. I suggested White Eskimo, and we hadn't thought of anything better, so we wrote that down and from then on that's who we were.'

'I had a few girlfriends here and there when I was really young, but I didn't have an actual girlfriend until I was twelve.'
– Harry

Dressed in their matching late-seventies, new wave-esque outfits of white shirts and black ties, White Eskimo blew away the competition to scoop the first prize. No one was more surprised than the band themselves, which isn't all that surprising given the short time they'd been together. But having now enjoyed the sweet taste of success, Harry, along with lead guitarist, Haydn, and drummer, Will, was keen to take things to the next level.

Unfortunately, this didn't suit everybody in the band and White Eskimo were forced into temporary hiatus while they broke in a new bassist. And with a paying gig in the offing, the new guy had to hit the ground running. 'A girl at my school said that her mum was getting married and wanted us to play at the wedding, so we rehearsed solidly for two days,' Harry explained. 'We had a set-list of about 25 songs that the bride had chosen, and we learnt the lot. We got paid £160, which worked out at £40 each. And we got free sandwiches – what more could you ask for?'

Having your singer set aside band duties in favour of a talent contest – albeit a very high-profile talent contest – would have ruffled the feathers of many an aspiring band member, but to then see him accept an offer to join another band on national television would have had them bad-mouthing their erstwhile colleague at every turn. But it seemed the rest of guys in White Eskimo were delighted for their friend. 'We've not split up but it's been difficult while he's away without a singer,' their bassist Nick Clough told the *Crewe Chronicle* in September 2010. 'We're happy for him and wish him all the best.'

Yet while Nick, Haydn and Will were happy to admit they were in regular contact with Harry while he was away on *The X Factor*, they were less willing to disclose whether Harry had given away any *X Factor* titbits. 'He said he's very busy and having a great time,' Haydn tactfully replied. 'Everyone here at school is behind him. It's great.' Harry's

head teacher, Denis Oliver, confirmed the school's support for their most famous pupil: 'Everyone here's supporting him – he's a popular lad. White Eskimo won Battle of the Bands here when he was in Year Ten. He's performed in a lot of assemblies.'

As with the other boys, it seems that Harry had always harboured ambitions of trying out for *The X Factor*, especially after watching Eoghan Quigg and Lloyd Daniels – who were the same age as he was – progress through to the 2009 live show finals. 'I was just like every other teenager at school, and had a weekend job in a bakery which was great. I worked for a lot of old ladies which was fun. I was in a band with some friends from school, and I had watched *X Factor* religiously when I was younger. I didn't know if I had what it took, and I was really nervous about actually taking the step and applying,' he later confided. 'In the end, my mum filled out the application form and sent it off for me – and I'm so grateful that she did. I often have those moments when I think, "What if she hadn't done that," or "What if so and so hadn't happened?"'

He recently recalled the moment when he discovered what his mum had been up to: 'It was like a family thing to watch [*The X Factor*] with my mum. We sat there on the finale the year before we were on it [2009] and I said, "I actually want to have a go at it one day." Then my mum actually put the application in and came up to me just a few weeks later and was like, "You've got an *X Factor* audition on Sunday", and I was like, "What?"'

Not surprisingly, Anne has found herself the centre of attention following her son's rise to stardom with One Direction – especially around the time of the UK release of 'What Makes You Beautiful'. During an interview with Radio One's Huw Stephens – in which revealed she'd be listening to the chart run-down later that afternoon to see where the single might land on the chart – Anne was asked to grade Harry on his 'motherly concerns'.

On remembering to call or text his mum he received a B+ and A* respectively, and he was also given a very respectable A- on his ability to cook a family meal. 'He's a very good cook,' said Anne. 'He likes his Tacos, so he's good at those – you know, he'll try his hand at anything. When he was younger he used to be a bit weird, he liked to make weird and wonderful things. When he was little he'd paint bread with food colouring and then toast it. He'd paint your picture on bread then toast it – very creative.'

Harry also shone when it came to remembering his mum's birthday and was given another A*, but when it came to tidying his room during a visit, there was obviously room for improvement as he was only rated a B-. Another A* was awarded for his grooming skills – even if he tended to use his fingers rather than a hairbrush – and when asked if he remembered to bring his mum a present back from his various travels, Anne gave him an A for the pair of shoes Harry had brought back from LA after the boys had been in America recording the album. He would have got an A* had he not returned from Sweden empty-handed.

> 'I didn't know if I had what it took to go on *The X Factor*, and I was really nervous about actually taking the step and applying.'
> – Harry

Gemma admitted to being equally bemused by seeing her baby brother in the television spotlight: 'The madness began at Harry's first *X Factor* audition for the judges,' she told *Mizz* magazine. 'It seemed quite funny – I was more excited about meeting Dermot O' Leary. The thought of Harry being on a show we'd watched every year was surreal. Every audition we'd cross our fingers that he'd get through, and the good news kept coming till we realised he had a shot at making it to Bootcamp.'

For his televised audition Harry chose to perform Stevie Wonder's 1976 Motown classic 'Isn't She Lovely', and while Louis Walsh – possibly sensing Harry's nervousness – expressed doubts as to whether he was ready to progress further, Simon and Nicole, who was again standing in for Dannii Minogue, thought otherwise.

'I couldn't believe how brave he was when his turn to go on stage came – it's my idea of hell,' Gemma said. 'His hands were visibly shaking, and backstage we all held our breath as he got a no from Louis Walsh. But, of course, Simon and Nicole said, "Yes." For the next few weeks, he only let mum and me listen to him as he practised in the bathroom. On the first day of Bootcamp we went to Wembley and I left him with the other nervous hopefuls. And you know the story from there.'

Indeed, we do, because despite his having satisfied Simon and Nicole at the auditions, like Liam, he was left crying in his coffee when his performance of Oasis' 'Stop Crying Your Heart Out' seemingly failed to impress the judges. But, of course, this was far from the end of Harry's *X Factor* adventure, for there was an earthbound angel waiting in the wings . . .

CHAPTER SIX

FINDING THE 'X'

'This for us is just unbelievable! We were all sat in the car
and I think it was Liam that said, "It feels like a dream and
that we're all going to wake up and our mums are gonna be like,
'Wake up, get ready for school,' kind of thing."'
– Zayn

The angel in question was none other than Nicole Scherzinger, as the former Pussycat Doll had recognised that some of the categories were much stronger than the others. She therefore suggested they compensate for this by raising the age limit for the older singers' group to 'Over-28s' and, seeing as the 'Groups' category was the weakest of the four, she also suggested that five of those rejected from the 'Boys' category and four from the 'Girls' should pool their talents. 'I practically put One Direction together with my hands tied behind my back,' she subsequently joked to fanpop.com.

'We invited these five guys back – they were the only five we cared about,' Simon Cowell told *Rolling Stone* magazine in April 2012. 'They looked like a group at that point, but obviously they had to come back for another section of the show where they performed together as a group for the first time. I was concerned whether five weeks [of rehearsal] was long enough, but they came back five weeks later and were absolutely sensational.'

Of course, all the unscheduled rearranging of the show's format was done behind closed doors, so Louis, Zayn, Liam, Niall and Harry were, naturally, all too distraught at having been eliminated to ponder why they'd been singled out from the other rejects and asked to remain behind, as Harry subsequently explained: 'They said we were wanted for interviews and, looking back, it's surprising that we didn't click on a bit quicker. We were all kind of like sat looking like [thinking], "Five teenage boys that they've kept back . . ." The best moment for me out of the whole thing was when we were told we were going to be put in a band together. I'd spoken to Louis, Zayn and Niall at Bootcamp and I remember thinking, "This is going to be a lot of fun."'

'For me, it was kind of like; I can either go home as a solo artist or I can continue in the competition in a group,' said Zayn. 'It was a bit of a no-brainer really.' The decision was also something of a no-brainer for Louis, who wasn't only relieved at being handed a lifeline, but also excited at the prospect of working on a new project for which Simon had chosen him. He would later reveal that he had always wanted to enter the show as part of band: 'Right at the start, before I auditioned for *The X Factor*, I actually put a few posts out on some really small forums saying, "I really want to go in a group this year," because I heard the success rate was higher in a group – but no one got back to me.'

The boys were obviously incredibly grateful for being given a second chance, and put their hearts and souls into making five work as one, as Niall explained: 'When we first got put together as a band Simon had told us that he'd given us a lifeline and he expected a lot in return. So not only were we doing this for ourselves, we felt like we owed him something too. He'd given us another chance and we needed to prove to him that he'd made the right decision, and we'd been a risk worth taking.'

'There's a lot of pressure on us – I mean there's gonna be millions of people watching and we've never done any live performing before.'
– Liam

Though the boys were unaware of it at the time, Simon had been assigned as mentor to the Groups category, which meant they'd be flying out to the music mogul's palatial villa in Marbella, to compete against Diva Fever, Hustle, Princes and Rogues, The Reason, Twem, F.Y.D, and of course, Belle Amie. Before that, however, they were given a week to bond, both as friends and bandmates.

Rather than put the boys up in a hotel, the producers allowed them to decide for themselves where they wanted to stay, for what was essentially going to be a team-building exercise. 'We'd been given this amazing opportunity to become a group, but the first thing that went through my mind after the excitement wore off was, "How the hell are we going to organise this when we're all from different places?"' Liam explained. 'Luckily Louis and Harry are a bit more organised than I am, and came up with the plan of staying in Cheshire because it was quite easy for everyone to get to.'

Thanks to Harry's stepdad's generosity, the boys set up camp in his guest bungalow – which, though having only one bedroom, had been recently refurbished and was equipped with all the mod cons – including a heated swimming pool. 'It was a new experience for all of us because it was like living in a student flat,' Harry explained. 'My mum and Robin completely left us to our own devices. We all put in some money and my mum put a load of food in the fridge and we were left to get on with it. I cooked dinner for us one night, [but] other than that I think we ate Super Noodles most days. We'd do ten minutes of singing practice, then play football for three hours, have a swim, [and then] drive to KFC. We were just messing around, but it was a really good way of getting to know each other's personalities.'

Though Simon had indeed given the boys a lifeline, it appeared as though that was

all he was willing to give them at this initial stage in their development, for it was left to them to come up with a name for their new band. While coming up with a name wasn't the most difficult hurdle facing the boys, considering everything else they had to worry about with the clock counting down towards their date with destiny at Judges' Houses, it was important they get it right. And they got it right first time, as Zayn explained: 'Harry came up with the name One Direction – because we were all going in the same direction as a group. Funnily enough, it was the first name we came up with, and we were like, "Brilliant, we'll go with that one."'

While the boys were all making an effort to get along, as with any five teenagers suddenly thrust together – in what, for four of them, were unfamiliar surroundings – it was only natural that some friendships developed quicker than others. Harry says that he and Louis hit it off from the get-go, while Liam – who enjoyed a similar 'bromance' with Zayn – was initially wary of Louis, because of his outgoing personality. 'At first I was a bit wary of him,' Liam admitted. 'He's a big influence on everyone in the band because he's the eldest and he has a sense of leadership. I'm more on the creative side, so I think we both want to lead in different ways, which meant it took us a bit longer to bond. As soon as we were honest with each other it worked, and we've ended up being really close mates.'

'There was never a quiet moment in the bungalow, and we talked about anything and everything, from past memories to the future,' Louis said of the adventure. 'We used to make a campfire every night and Niall would play his guitar and we'd sing along. I think it is incredible how we'd met so recently and within a week we felt like best friends. It wasn't forced in any way, it just happened naturally.'

Niall believes this ad-hoc bonding session to be one of his most treasured experiences of being in One Direction: 'That's where it all started for us. We used to play football in the garden and mess around. We kept telling ourselves that we'd get up the next day at nine and start rehearsing, but instead we'd get up at twelve and start watching TV.'

As Zayn had a few things to sort out at home, he didn't arrive at the bungalow until three days after the others had moved in and, on walking through the door and seeing how much the others had bonded in so short a time, he was left feeling out of the loop. However, while he was the 'newcomer', so to speak, the awkwardness didn't last long. 'Luckily, the lads are really outgoing and fun, so I soon felt like a part of the group,' he explained. 'We'd sit around the campfire singing and watch TV and eat. We were kind of getting to know each other without even realising that we were getting to know each other.'

While the boys would have undoubtedly been bursting with excitement as they took their seats aboard the plane bound for Marbella on Spain's sunshine coast, they – like the guys and girls making up the other bands – would also have been extremely nervous, for they each knew that their seven-day sojourn under the sun wasn't going to be a holiday. For they were about to enter the Kingmaker's lair, where one mistake could undo all the hard work they'd put in so far, and their dreams would evaporate like the early morning mist drifting down from the Sierra Blanca.

'We really didn't have a clue what we were doing, so we basically headed out to Marbella hoping for the best but with no idea how we would do,' Niall later confided about their collective state of mind. 'Spain gave us more time to get to know each other and see what people are like in different situations. We took everything really seriously, but we also made sure we had fun. We wanted to make the most of it. We were probably the loudest band there – at any rate people were often telling us to be quiet.'

> '**Harry came up with the name One Direction – because we were all going in the same direction as a group.**'
> – Zayn

'That trip to Spain was the first time I'd been abroad, and we were in one of the nicest places ever, so I'll never forget being there,' Zayn added reflectively. 'I didn't own a passport before the show. In fact, I'd never even been to London before my audition. [But] Marbella was probably the time when we actually felt like a group. It was the first time we auditioned as a band and sang in front of Simon, so we really pulled it together.'

While the boys took a no-nonsense approach when it came to filming and rehearsing, like any other teenagers abroad for the first time, they couldn't resist testing the boundaries, or the patience, of *The X Factor*'s staff. The mischievous Zayn says that he and Louis often sneaked out of their hotel 'just to get away from things', and, having grabbed a pizza, the pair would then head off and find a secluded spot on the beach somewhere and watch the world go by. 'Going out to Marbella was another really good time for us,' Louis agreed. 'We all bonded even more and it was so nice being in the sun. We had fun, ate a lot of pizza, and because Niall can speak really good Spanish, he could translate things for us.'

Harry has admitted to being lost for words when Niall sang the lyrics to 'What Makes You Beautiful' in Spanish, but it's doubtful whether his familiarity with the local lingo extended to his being able to name the creatures which inhabited that particular stretch of the Mediterranean Sea. Louis found out to his painful cost that it's best to keep an eye out for sea urchins – or erizos de mar – when wading in the ocean. 'My foot swelled up incredibly,' he said, grimacing at the memory. 'It was embarrassing to be seen hobbling along, and the first time I was shown on screen it looked absolutely massive. The timing wasn't exactly great.'

Indeed it wasn't, because Louis's encounter with the lurking sea urchin came just a few hours before the boys were due to give their make-or-break performance in front of Simon and his guest judge, Sinitta (who'd been Simon's first signing way back in 1986), and the injury was deemed severe enough for a trip to casualty. Thankfully, however, a sea urchin's quills are more painful than poisonous, and a limping Louis was discharged within the hour. He was able to take his place beside the others when the boys performed LA rockers Ednaswap's 1995 hit 'Torn', which, of course, was also

a massive hit for Natalie Imbruglia – who was serving as Dannii's sounding board while she cast her eye over Matt, Aiden, Paije Richardson, and the other male soloists at her home in Melbourne.

While Simon thought the boys' performance a 'little bit timid', as they chose to take turns at singing the verses rather than reworking the song to show what they could do as a group, he obviously saw enough to satisfy him that his decision to bring them to his home had been the right one. 'They're cool; they're relevant,' he enthused for the camera. 'This is going to be a hard decision.'

Of course, we know now that it wasn't really a 'hard decision' for Simon to reach, as he explained to *Rolling Stone*: 'When they came to my house in Spain and performed, after about a millionth of a second. I tried to keep a straight face for a bit of drama for the show. I remember sitting next to this girl [Sinitta] who I was working with. The second they left, I jumped out of my chair and said, "These guys are incredible!" They just had it. They had this confidence. They were fun. They worked out the arrangements themselves. They were like a gang of friends, and kind of fearless as well.'

'On the day we were due to hear whether or not we were through to the live finals everyone was up really early for breakfast and the atmosphere was incredibly tense,'

said Niall. 'We didn't find out our fate until late in the afternoon, and the boys and I spent all day talking about how we thought we'd done, while also trying to have a laugh to take our mind off things.'

Simon, in his typical poker-faced fashion, kept the boys dangling on a hook for the benefit of the TV cameras before informing them – and the millions watching at home – of his decision: 'My head is saying it's a risk, and my heart is saying you deserve a shot,' he told them. 'And that's why it's been difficult, so I've made a decision. Guys, I've gone with my heart – you're through.'

Niall later revealed that standing there waiting for the verdict had been one of the longest moments of his young life: 'Hearing a "yes" would change my life forever, and my mind kept going back to the performance – replaying it in my head and wondering if we could have done it better. It's so hard to read Simon's face, so it could have gone either way, and when he said he was putting us through I wanted to leap about ten feet in the air.'

Before heading for London and moving into the *X Factor* house along with the other finalists, however, upon their return from Spain the boys went home to spend time with their families. While leaving their respective homes, families and friends behind had

'It's so hard to read Simon's face, so it could have gone either way, and when he said he was putting us through I wanted to leap about ten feet in the air.'

– Niall

affected some more than others – notably Louis and Zayn, who are both particularly close to their mums – this was what they'd each been praying for, ever since sending off for the application forms.

'When we arrived in London we stayed in hotels for a couple of days while they finished getting the house ready,' Niall said. 'Then we moved in, and when I saw our room I wondered how we'd all fit in there. I'm very clean, and I don't like my things being out of place, but Louis is the messiest person I've ever met. He'd just leave everything on the floor and I used to have to clean up after him!'

Despite the fact that he'd already experienced the pungent pitfalls of living cheek by jowl with the other boys at Harry's stepdad's bungalow before departing for Spain, having to share a room with them in the contestants' house was a bit of an eye-opener for Liam, as he revealed: 'The room was tiny, and we spent all day together too. We all found little ways to have some time to ourselves, and that was very important. I used to get in and go straight to bed, but the other guys used to stay up a lot later, so I was always telling them off for waking me up.'

'We had a lot of luggage and there was too much stuff in the room, so it ended up being a bit grim,' said Harry. 'We did try to keep [things] tidy, but the longer we were in the show the more stuff we accumulated, and the room seemed to get smaller and smaller.'

Having never had to share a room with anyone before – let alone four relative strangers – Zayn found the whole experience of living in each other's pockets quite unnerving. 'It soon became pretty horrible. It smelt like five teenage boys and it was so messy,' he groaned. 'I'm quite organised and I like to know where things are, but most of the others just didn't care and they'd throw things everywhere. There would be socks all over the floor, underwear hanging from light bulbs and dirty plates. It wasn't nice.'

> **'We were getting through each week and more and more fans were coming outside the studio and I'm just a normal, nineteen-year-old guy – from Doncaster of all places!'**
> **– Louis**

While it's open to question what would have become of Niall, Zayn, Liam, Louis and Harry had there not been a surfeit of talented older singers in the 2010 *X Factor*, few can argue that they added a new dynamic to the whole competition. Indeed, from the moment they took to the stage to perform Coldplay's massive transatlantic 2008 hit 'Viva La Vida' on the opening live show, the smart money was on One Direction to scoop the £1 million recording contract.

The saddest moment for Zayn during his time on *The X Factor* came with the passing of his grandfather, Walter, and it is a testament to his character that he was able to carry on in the competition. 'He'd been ill for quite a while, and he'd had a few strokes, so in a way I knew it was coming,' Zayn later revealed. 'It was horrible not being at home around the time it all happened, but I was so glad he got to see us sing "You Are So Beautiful" on the show [as] it was his favourite song.'

While Simon would have already been quietly confident – having seen the boys coast through the opening live show – that his gamble was going to pay dividends, on hearing the crescendo of screams that threatened to lift the roof from its rafters following their performance of Kelly Clarkson's 2009 US Number One 'My Life Would Suck Without You' on week two, he could contain himself no more: 'You are, in my opinion, the most exciting pop band in the country. There is something absolutely right,' he brazenly declared, as if daring Dannii, Cheryl, or Louis to challenge him. It was around this time that the girls in the audience began to realise that their lives would suck without One Direction, and a fair percentage of those living within the west London area began laying siege to the *X Factor* house and TV studio.

'A fortnight ago, I was just an ordinary lad from Wolverhampton [and] now there are screaming girls outside my window,' a bewildered Liam told the Wolverhampton *Express & Star*. 'There are girls stood out by the gates of the studio, 24/7. You only have to walk past and when they see you they just start screaming. It's great! They

'You get such a massive buzz from being there singing in front of the judges and the audience.'
– Harry

will pass you gifts through the fence. A couple of the lads have had bracelets. I had a teddy bear the other day off a girl. And someone gave us cakes the once.' And it wasn't only gaggles of screaming girls the boys had to get used to laying in wait for them. 'It's weird when we go out and get chased by paparazzi,' Liam told his local paper. 'There will be about eight photographers there just taking photos of you walking down the street. It's very weird. It's hard to get used to, but it's cool.'

Though 1D Mania had been gathering momentum in schoolyards up and down the country, week six was the first clear indication that life after *The X Factor* was never going to be the same for One Direction. For this was the week that boy band heavyweights Take That – giving their first public performance following prodigal son Robbie Williams's return – as well as Westlife and JLS, would all be performing live in the studio. Each of the three bands had their fans gathering outside, and the show's anxious producers were forced to call in the riot police to deal with the horde of screaming schoolgirls who'd laid siege to the north London studio where the live shows were being filmed, in the desperate hope of catching a glimpse of their idols. Indeed, such was the turnout at Fountain Studios that the road outside the studio was blocked to oncoming traffic. Louis, for one, found the whole experience quite bewildering, as he subsequently revealed on *One Direction: A Year In The Making*: 'We were getting through each week and more and more fans were coming outside the studio and I'm just a normal, nineteen-year-old guy – from Doncaster of all places!'

During his aforementioned visit home in the week leading up to *The X Factor* semi-finals, Louis admitted to his local newspaper – the *Doncaster Free Press* – that the strain was beginning to get to him and the other lads: 'The pressure is really on, we've not had a minute. We're constantly working and improving our vocals. We've been doing eighteen-hour days and have been in the studio until 2:00am so it's really tough. We don't know from week to week if we are going to get through because there's been a lot of surprises. All I remember thinking was that we needed to smash our "save me" song so that we could stay in the competition.'

Two days after claiming their place in *The X Factor* semi-finals alongside Matt Cardle, Rebecca Ferguson, and Cher Lloyd, with their faultless renditions of Rihanna's recent transatlantic smash, 'Only Girl (In The World)', and Snow Patrol's 2006 hit 'Chasing Cars', the boys went on a whistle-stop promotional tour of Doncaster, Bradford, Holmes Chapel and Wolverhampton to meet and greet their home-grown fans. Harry admitted to being blown away by the reception which greeted their arrival in Holmes Chapel – the village had been adorned with banners, balloons and signs saying 'Welcome Home Harry'. 'Everyone's been brilliant,' he said. 'It's a weird and wonderful feeling to have your home town all rooting for you.'

There was an even bigger crowd awaiting their arrival in Wolverhampton, where the boys were set to perform a short open-air set in Queen's Square in front of an estimated four thousand ecstatic fans. Indeed, such was the crowd's enthusiasm that people who were gathered at the front of the stage were injured when those to the rear suddenly surged forwards to get a closer glimpse of the band. 'Wolverhampton was absolutely awesome, the crowd were absolutely amazing,' local lad Liam later said in their *X Factor* video diary. 'Five thousand people were there waiting for us and we went on stage and did three songs and it was the best gig any of us had ever done.'

Of course, what made it all the more amazing was that while the excitement and the attendant pressures of appearing on *The X Factor* live stage had proved too much for F.Y.D, Diva Fever, and Belle Amie – who had all been voted off by the fourth week to leave One Direction as Simon's last remaining act – the boys appeared to be taking everything in their stride. Though they admitted to having the odd argument, the fallouts usually blew over quickly. 'Because we're around each other so often it's like arguing with your siblings,' Louis reasoned. 'You fall out with them, go away and have a bit of a paddy, then come back and get over it.'

'I think every band has arguments,' Liam added. 'But the funny thing is you just get over them really quickly. They last about five minutes. You just get over it because you know we're all going for the same thing so you just put your differences aside and get on with it.' And Zayn revealed that he'd found the perfect means of apologising to the others should his occasional outburst or tantrum rub anyone up the wrong way. 'I like making up by going to McDonald's, and buying a takeaway for the lads just to show I'm [still] their mate.'

CHAPTER SEVEN

GOTTA BE THEM

'Going down to the studios on the Sunday morning of the
final was so weird because we all knew that it was the last time
we'd leave the [*X Factor*] house as part of the competition. They were
already moving stuff out of the house as we left, so it looked surreal
and not the way we had known it.'

– Louis

On Sunday evening, 12 December – with a television audience estimated at close to eighteen million waiting with collective baited breath – One Direction faced Rebecca Ferguson and Matt Cardle in the triangulated finale for the 2010 *X Factor* crown.

The previous evening the boys had given a brilliant performance of Elton John's 1970 Top Ten hit 'Your Song', as well as duetting with Robbie Williams on the latter's 1999 Number One 'She's The One'. Simon praised the boys for having given 1,000 percent, and said that it had been 'an absolute pleasure' working with them: 'I really hope people bother to pick up the phone, [and] put you through to tomorrow because you deserve to be there.'

For the final, the boys chose to perform Ednaswap's 'Torn', as they had done at Simon's house in Marbella. Only this time, it was faultless – absolutely faultless. 'It's funny that the same song, "Torn", ended up being our first and last performance on the series,' Niall reflected. 'It seemed as though we'd come full circle.'

However, despite the ear-piercing crescendo of screams which threatened to lift the studio roof from its stanchions, their efforts – which, judging from the audience reaction, appeared to match Matt's reworking of Katy Perry's 2010 US Number One 'Firework' and Rebecca's smouldering rendition of the Eurythmics' 1983 hit 'Sweet Dreams (Are Made Of This)' – the boys were surprisingly eliminated, having polled some twelve percent less of the vote than second-placed Rebecca.

'We were standing on stage with Matt and Rebecca, and they called Matt's name out first. Then they called Rebecca's and we were so deflated,' Liam recalled. 'We hadn't experienced that situation before, because our name had always been called out on the right side when the votes came in. When I watched it back on TV it seemed like Dermot waited ages to read out Rebecca's name, but when I was there it felt like no time at all. As soon as Dermot reads out Rebecca's name you can see all our faces drop, and our fans in the audience kind of slumped. It wasn't that we believed the hype when people said we were going to win, but we couldn't help but hope.'

Though the boys were visibly upset upon hearing that their race had been run, they were determined to put on a brave face in front of the cameras. 'It's been absolutely incredible,' Louis told Dermot. 'For me the highlight was when we first sang together at the Judges' Houses. That was unbelievable. We have done our absolute best.' 'We're definitely going to stay together,' Zayn added, much to the delight of the audience. 'This is not the last of One Direction.'

The boys were also magnanimous in defeat, and wished Matt and Rebecca well in the head-to-head performance before taking a salutary bow to the audience and judges and departing from the stage. 'We were up against two amazing people,' Zayn said on *XTRA Factor*. 'And I said to the lads if we go out now, I'm happy to go out to Rebecca and Matt because they're both incredible.'

When *Digital Spy* asked Harry what had been his outstanding *X Factor* highlight, he didn't even hesitate and told the website: 'When we walked in and saw the studio for the first time. Then, when us five stood behind the doors for the first time on the live show, for that first song – for me that was the best moment. That was where we were actually doing it, the real thing, for the first time. That was a big moment.'

> **'It wasn't that we believed the hype when people said we were going to win, but we couldn't help but hope.'**
> **– Liam**

Failure is difficult to deal with, and both the audience and the viewing millions sitting at home could have been forgiven for thinking that, other than spotting the odd photo of them on stage during the forthcoming X Factor Live Tour in one of the tabloids, this was the last the world would hear of One Direction. Indeed, the tabloid showbiz columnists appeared infinitely more interested in hearing Simon's reaction to his protégés' apparent failure to live up to his billing, rather than in what the future held for One Direction. Simon, however, was having none of it and kept his responses focused on the boys: 'I am absolutely gutted for them,' he told *The Star*. 'All I can say is this is just the beginning for these boys.'

Cheryl Cole echoed Simon's sentiments: 'You can't help but think, "How big are these guys going to be?"' she enthused. 'It's mind-blowing.' And for once, it seemed Louis Walsh was in complete agreement with his long-running *X Factor* antagonist. 'They could be the new Beatles, the new Take That, or the new Westlife. Massive,' he enthused.

Of course, it wasn't only the judges and studio guests who were expecting One Direction to shrug off what was, after all, a minor setback and carry on. Louis's mum, Johannah, told reporters that she and the rest of the Tomlinson family wouldn't be expecting Louis to be returning to the family home in Doncaster after the excitement of the last few months. 'Whatever happened in the final, they wanted to stay together as a group,' she said, while Louis's equally proud dad looked on. 'They know they are

going to have to work hard to be successful. They know that from doing ten weeks of eighteen-hour days since they have been in *The X Factor*. They have been working much harder than if they had been in their old jobs.' She added: 'Louis said the best thing about *The X Factor* was the day Simon put them together, because he made four new friends.'

'[It's] like a whirlwind, and when you're in the middle of it it's so hard to process it properly,' Zayn recalled of *The X Factor* experience. 'Everything is going so fast and you're suddenly standing on red carpets ad meeting famous people and singing to millions. When I look back on it now I realise how full on it was. You don't watch TV; you don't know what's going on in the outside world. All that matters to you is the competition, so you can feel a bit detached from reality.'

Liam was definitely left with a surreal feeling as he posed for a photo with his hero, Robbie Williams. 'I thanked him and told him that if it wasn't for him I probably wouldn't [have been] in the show,' he gushed. 'He gave us great advice about staying down to earth, and he made so much sense.' Zayn was equally impressed with Robbie, even though he admitted to having never been much of a fan. 'I was converted as soon as I met him,' he revealed. 'He has an aura about him and it's very evident when he walks into a room. While everyone else had Rihanna, Christine Aguilera, and Will.i.am singing with them, Robbie stayed with us all day and got to know us – that's why you could feel the chemistry on stage.'

Though the boys enjoyed basking in the backstage afterglow, the show was over, the celebrities, fellow *X Factor* finalists, studio audience, and everyone else except their families had gone home, and Matt's beaming face would be the one staring up from the front pages of the following morning's tabloids.

'We're definitely going to stay together. This is not the last of One Direction.'
– Zayn

As the five of them made their way up to Simon's dressing room to learn their fate, each of them must have thought this was the end of the line – at least in terms of being given the red carpet treatment, and feted everywhere they went. For Simon had said time and time again over the past ten weeks that he only ever signed winners.

Zayn came off stage promising himself that he wouldn't cry, but his resolve crumbled on seeing Harry bawling his eyes out. 'I think as much as anything we were crying because the show was coming to an end, and we were used to having the safety and security of it and knowing what we were going to be doing each day, and all of a sudden it was over – even if our career wasn't.

'We got called up to Simon's dressing room and then came the classic Simon moment,' Zayn said of their late-night tête-à-tête with Mr. Cowell, which, as they made their way upstairs, must have seemed like a summons from a disapproving headmaster. 'We all sat there and he was looking at us, and it felt like we were back at [the] Judges' Houses again. Then all of a sudden he said: "You were great on the show. Sony are going to sign you up in the morning. You're going to be all right, don't worry about coming third."'

'I tried to stay as calm as possible, but on the inside I was terrified,' Harry added. 'As soon as Simon told us we had a record deal and I started crying again and I sat there thinking, "Why am I crying? If this works out it's going to totally change my life." My life had already changed so much, but this was the moment that told me I didn't have to go back to doing what I did before – at least not for a while. I couldn't wait to tell my family the news, but of course we had to keep it quiet. I went back downstairs to the bar area because there was a little party going on, and I think my parents could tell from the look on my face what had happened.'

Liam also recalled the moment of truth when they were summoned up to Simon's office: 'The atmosphere was incredibly tense, and we were all looking at each other nervously. We wanted more than anything to stay together as a band and record an album, but of course, Simon made us wait a bit before he delivered the news. It was like being back at the Judges' Houses, because he was saying how much he liked us, but not giving us a definite answer. Then he told us that he was signing us and we were in complete shock.'

'Simon told us that he was signing us and we were in complete shock.'
– Liam

Little could the boys have known, however, that Simon had been picturing that particular scenario in his mind's eye for the past ten weeks or so, and while he would have no doubt preferred it if they'd won the final, he'd long-since made his mind up that he was the man to steer One Direction in the right direction. However, as he subsequently told *Rolling Stone*, he was perfectly willing to listen to all sides of the argument: 'They [the boys] had their own views and they all brought something special to the table. I thought, "As long as we can get the right record, they've got a great shot." This was such an important signing, we let three or four of the Sony labels make a presentation'.

Though the boys had told only their nearest and dearest about Simon's proposal, news that they were signing a £2 million deal with Syco was already circulating on the internet by the time they lifted their heads from their pillows the following morning – as was a download of the song 'More Than This', which the label had been intending to release as One Direction's Christmas single, if they'd won.

'We moved out of the *X Factor* house the morning after the final, and it was a strange atmosphere,' Niall recalled. 'Our room was such a mess. There was stuff absolutely everywhere, and we basically had to pack three months of clothes in an hour. There were some Mercedes vans waiting outside for us, and I was like, "This is the life! I could get used to this."'

The next few days were taken up with management meetings, while in the evenings they made guest appearances at various clubs around London. 'The reception we got in the clubs was amazing because we were out there doing proper shows with a set-list of songs,' said Liam. 'We could have carried on doing that for weeks but then Christmas rolled around, and I think we were all in need of a bit of a break after the madness of recent months.'

Niall arrived back in Mullingar wanting nothing more than to sleep for a month, but as he'd been too busy in London in the run-up to Christmas, he had to get his Christmas shopping done. As Ireland has a proud musical history – what with their record in the Eurovision Song Contest, and the chart success of Boyzone and Westlife – the people of Mullingar had been following Niall every step of the way and were naturally thrilled at being able to congratulate him on his return. 'People kept coming up to me in the street, and all over the place there were posters saying, "Best of luck, Niall," and "Good luck One Direction."'

Zayn also experienced what it was like to be a home-grown celebrity while out Christmas shopping with his sister, Doniya. 'I didn't realise how recognisable I'd become, but literally one person clocked me and the next thing the entire shopping centre came to a standstill. There was a queue of people waiting to take photos of me and I was like, "What the hell is going on?" My sister found it really weird as well because I'm her little brother. Sometimes I think it's even harder for your family to get their heads around it than it is for you.

'I can't even begin to describe what it was like when we all stood on stage together for the first night of the tour in Birmingham.' – Harry

While his family and friends were incredibly supportive during his time on the show, Zayn said that his extended family, including aunties, uncles and cousins, found it difficult to know how to act around him once One Direction started getting publicity. 'If they do something for me they don't want me to think they're doing it just because I'm in the band, when actually it's the same things they've always done for me,' he said wistfully. 'Fame can do funny things to people's minds, and sometimes [they] overcompensate when they don't need to.'

Though Zayn says he'd never had much of a problem with the ladies before his stint on *The X Factor*, he now suddenly found that the girls at school who'd previously ignored him were being very friendly. 'It does make you realise what the fame card does for you,' he added. 'But I'm very aware [of] who is good for me and who isn't, and I know who I can trust.'

Louis said that being something of a celebrity didn't make Christmas feel any different, but it seemed that not everyone in Doncaster was happy that one of their own had achieved success, as he revealed: 'When I got back to Doncaster I heard that a few guys I knew were talking about me behind my back, and saying that I didn't deserve to be where I was. Certainly I've had a lot of luck to be in the place I am now, but at the end of the day I worked really, really hard, so regardless of whether or not they think I'm good enough, I am here for a reason.'

'Over Christmas I missed the boys quite a lot, but at the same time it was great just to relax and see my family,' said Harry. 'Loads of my friends wanted to catch up, so things

were quite busy, but I didn't want people to think that I'd changed and I didn't have time for them or whatever.' While the majority of his friends were thrilled for him, he found a few green-eyed monsters lurking in the Holmes Chapel bushes: 'Some people have made comments and distanced themselves from me without actually letting me know. When you've been close to someone it's hard when they start acting that way towards you. I'm not going to chase after people and beg them to be my friend, but I wouldn't want them to think I don't care, because I do.'

> 'For me the best part of being in the band is the time we spend in the studio.'
>
> – Zayn

Though all the boys had missed their families during the competition, Zayn, having been something of a home bird prior to going on *The X Factor*, perhaps missed his mum, dad, and sisters the most – especially in light of his grandfather's death. 'I appreciate getting to spend time with my family so much more now, because when I do get to go home it's so fleeting that I make the most of every minute,' he said. 'That's what made Christmas so nice [because] we spent as much time together as we could and had a brilliant time.'

However, having said that, Zayn found that he was missing his 1D family – as did Louis, Liam, Niall and Harry, despite their having lived in each other's shadows for the best part of three months, smelly socks and all! 'We were like big girls, saying, "I miss you. Are you okay? What are you up to? Love you,"' he chuckled. 'We'd spent so much time together that it felt weird to be apart. It was like being away from my family all over again in a way.'

Louis's mum Johannah Tomlinson recently told *Sugarscape* that the friendships her son and the other boys in the band have forged with each other are totally genuine and not something put on for the benefit of the TV cameras: 'People assume that bands are mates for all the publicity, but actually they're like that all the time. They seek each other out on their days off and they spend time with each other out of choice. It's very natural. You'd never think they were put together, it's so lucky . . . They don't take it for granted. If you watch their performances, you can see how in awe Louis is of the situation, you see him exhale – blow out, they don't take it for granted. They're blown away.'

There's no arguing that 2010 had been one a hell of a year for One Direction, and as the chimes of Big Ben rang out the changes to usher in 2011, Louis, Zayn, Niall, Liam and Harry would have all surely raised their glasses to the heavens in salute. But of course, the coming year promised to be even more exciting, for not only would they be accompanying Matt Cardle, Rebecca Ferguson, and the other *X Factor* live show finalists on the X Factor Live tour, which was set to commence with four sell-out shows at the Birmingham LG Arena over the weekend of 19–20 February, they would also begin recording their debut album for Syco.

'LA is something else. Everyone you see looks like they're famous.' – Harry

'We knew we had a busy January ahead of us, and we were ready for it,' Louis explained. 'I'd had a really good rest, but I missed performing live and I was kind of itching to get back into it. January was also spent talking about plans for the future, and we were set to start working on our album, so whenever we had a spare moment we were coming up with ideas about how we wanted it to sound.'

'We spent most of January either doing gigs or starting work on the album in various recording studios,' Zayn added. 'For me the best part of being in the band is the time we spend in the studio. The studio is much more fun when you're in a band because you've always got someone to mess around, play games and do some writing with.'

The boys were so thrilled at the prospect of going into the studio and pooling ideas for songs that would make up the new album that they didn't stop to think which studio they would be using. 'We'd gone to have dinner with our manager, Richard Griffiths, at his house,' Liam explained. 'We all left our phones in the car so we'd look professional, but when we sat down to eat, he started talking about us going to LA [to do some recording for the album]. We couldn't believe it. My dad always said to me that if we ever got told we were going to LA he wanted to be the first to hear about it. My first reaction was to reach for me phone [but] I didn't have it!'

Harry and Niall had already visited America on family holidays, but neither one could have imagined that, the next time they boarded a plane bound for the land of the brave and home of the free, they'd be doing so to go to Los Angeles to record an album. 'LA is something else,' Harry beamed. 'Everyone you see looks like they're famous. We did some recording in this really cool complex where there were loads of different things going on. In one studio they were recording the backing vocals for Glee, and then Randy Jackson's office was 100 metres away, so we went to meet him.'

While the City of Angels certainly lived up to Zayn's 'sugar-coated' expectations, he found the experience of entering America somewhat less pleasant, as he later explained: 'All the lads went through passport control fine, then a woman stopped me, called over our tour manager, Paul, and said, "There's a problem with him. He needs to go back."' Zayn's name had flagged up on the system as it was similar to that of someone the American authorities were looking for in connection with terrorist activities. He was led off to a room while the rest of the band looked on helpless, but thankfully the matter was eventually sorted out and he was allowed through.

'When you look out into the audience and someone's got your name on a banner, it doesn't really sink in that it's yours.' – Liam

Subsequently, LAX's beleaguered US Marshal's Department – who'd had their hands full trying to hold off the horde of screaming girls who'd descended on the airport, anxious to catch a glimpse of their heroes – told the band that it 'wasn't safe' for them to engage in a meet and greet session. Though disappointed at not being able to thank their fans in person, Harry and Niall took to their Twitter accounts to apologise to their fans for the confusion: 'Sorry that we couldn't stop at LAX guys . . . the US Marshall's said it wasn't safe,' Harry tweeted. 'We all wanted to come see you .x.' While Niall wrote: 'So sorry guys! US marshals said it wasn't safe for us to come out! Thank you for comin to LAX to see us! We heard there was 600 of u! Love u. Lets go USA , this is soooo exciting! The reception we got at LAX thank you all soo much!'

While One Direction's experiences at LAX were unnerving, they were nothing compared to the scenes which greeted the boys' arrival at Heathrow. 'We were told that there were about 200 people waiting for us, so we were ready to sign autographs and things. But when we walked out this whole swarm of people came towards us, so we had to run back inside the airport,' Zayn explained. 'There was no plan, so we just held onto each other and ran.'

'Airport security came to help us, but there were loads of paparazzi there as well so it was crazy,' Niall said, picking up the story. 'I'm really claustrophobic, so I was panicking a bit when we had to run through everyone and then hide in this parking booth. I was so relieved when the police riot van came and got us. I still can't believe that happened – it feels like it was all some kind of mad dream.'

The airport's hapless security team tried to smuggle the boys out through a side door, but the fans spotted them and they were completely mobbed. 'When the police van arrived we had to run from this parking booth we were hiding in and try to get into

the back of it,' added Liam, who was accidentally hit in the face during the scrum. 'But someone had hold of my hood so I ended up being squashed against the side of the van. In the end, someone grabbed me and threw me into the back of the van. We drove off with lights flashing and sirens sounding, so it was all quite dramatic.'

The boys were beginning to realise what it meant to be in the eye of the hurricane, but they didn't even have time to catch their breath, as the opening date of the X Factor Live Tour was looming large on the horizon. 'Light Structures in Wakefield is a massive warehouse where they built the set we'd be using on the tour,' Niall explained. 'We'd [already] rehearsed in London with a live band, and also learnt new dance moves and ways to move around the stage, [and] we went through the whole performance over and over without an audience. It was quite weird performing to no one, but it was brilliant for us because it got us used to how everything would look on the opening night.'

> 'I appreciate getting to spend time with my family so much more now, because when I do get to go home it's so fleeting that I make the most of every minute.'
> – Zayn

'Putting everything we'd learnt into practice was the ultimate pay-off for all the hard work we'd done,' said Harry. 'I can't even begin to describe what it was like when we all stood on stage together for the first night of the tour in Birmingham. I think that first arena performance was different to anything else we'd ever done in terms of how much energy we put into it, and how much we moved around the stage. It felt almost natural being [up] there, even though it was also completely and utterly surreal. There were times when we all looked at each other, and I could tell we were all thinking the same thing – "This is incredible!"'

'The reaction we got was unbelievable, and people of all ages were screaming at us all and having the best time,' Zayn recalled of the experience. 'A year ago the thought of being on stage in front of that many people would have been enough to make me physically sick, but now I go out and walk around the stage and I feel so much more confident. It's absolutely the best feeling.'

Liam was especially thrilled, given that Birmingham was in effect his home town: 'The first night was phenomenal and took us completely by surprise,' he revealed. 'Nothing could have prepared us for what we faced that first night. We were waiting to go on stage and we had our earpieces in, so we could hear some screams but not very clearly. We weren't expecting anything mega, and then we popped out of the man lifts [the lifts which brought the boys up from beneath the stage] and we could see all the banners and One Direction T-shirts, and people screaming. When you look out into the audience and someone's got your name on a banner, it doesn't really sink in that it's yours.'

'I definitely think all of the rehearsing paid off,' Louis reasoned. 'When I watch our performances from *The X Factor*, anything that required a little bit of movement or energy – like "Only Girl In The World" – looks so different from how we perform it now. I think we've all learnt to have a bit more stage presence and we're much more confident. Harry has always been the most comfortable on stage, but I think we've all caught up with him now.'

The *Guardian* described the mass hysteria which greeted the boys' arrival on stage at the O2 Arena, only to then criticise their performance by opining that 'they make mid-

'We had a quite few hotel parties on tour. There was always a private bar where we could chill out and chat after shows.'
– Zayn

period Boyzone look like the Rat Pack'. The boys would have undoubtedly found such comments hurtful, but they were careful not to let it affect them too much. 'It's a shame when people aren't supportive, because at the end of the day we're just nice, ordinary guys, and we've come from nothing and worked really hard to be here,' Liam later mused. 'If they were in this position, they'd feel exactly the same way. I remember being on stage in Birmingham and the lights were on the audience, and I was looking out at them thinking, "This is my job. I don't care what it takes; I'm not going to stop doing this."'

Of course, all work and no play makes for a dull day – especially for five high-spirited teenagers – and it wasn't long before they started to bring out the mischievous side in everyone else. But as the high jinx was always good-natured they tended to get away with it, because the people who were supposed to be overseeing them whilst on tour couldn't help but join in the fun. Indeed, the only time they did cross the line was when Louis started a fruit fight in the dressing room in Sheffield, as the culprit himself subsequently revealed: 'It all started with me trying to throw an apple core into the bin and missing, which somehow turned into everyone picking up apples and throwing

'I loved the tour so much I never wanted it to stop. I didn't even get homesick.'
– Harry

them at the wall as hard as they could. We were sharing a room with the other male artists and we all started picking up any fruit we could find, so there were oranges all over the floor and bits of pear all over the tables.'

As not everyone in the touring party was of legal age, the after-show parties were obviously rather more laidback, as Zayn explains: 'We had a quite few hotel parties on tour. There was always a private bar where we could chill out and chat after shows. It was nice doing things like that, and also just being myself and playing games.'

Niall also enjoyed the odd drink as a means of unwinding afterwards. 'I went down to the bar most nights, but we weren't having wild parties, we were just hanging out and talking. When you come off stage you're still buzzing, and I find it hard to go straight to bed so that was my way of winding down after the show. We had a few parties in the run-up to the end of the tour, and the wrap party itself was good Craic. A few people

from our management and record label came down, as well as our friends and family. I stayed at the party till four in the morning, and I had to leave the hotel at five to get to the airport to fly home, so I didn't get any sleep at all.'

One band member who couldn't go wild and party every night – even if he'd wanted to – was Liam, as he has to strictly monitor what he eats and drinks. 'With only the one kidney I have to be careful with things like salt, protein and alcohol, so I guess that's led to me being the sensible one. I think even when I'm old enough to drink I won't. My plan is to learn to drive, so I can ferry the other lads around and act as security when we go out.'

Liam thoroughly enjoyed himself on tour – even when he ripped his trousers from the belt line all the way down his leg just before going out on stage – but he was still relieved that the tour was finally over. 'We felt happy and relieved,' he said. 'Much as we loved the tour, we did around 60 shows, so we were all pleased to be having a bit of a break afterwards.'

'We couldn't believe the size of the crowds who came along. Everywhere we looked there were massive crowds of people.' – Louis

Though Harry was set to go skiing in Courchevel in France with Louis and some friends, he said he was enjoying himself so much on the tour that he didn't want to get off the merry-go-round, and would have happily embarked on another tour had Simon so wished. 'I loved the tour so much I never wanted it to stop,' he admitted. 'I didn't even get homesick because we were so busy we didn't get time to think about it, but I actually felt really guilty about that.'

Aside from expressing themselves on stage, the boys were also able to recount their experiences and convey their thoughts on paper. 'We were all really chuffed when we were told we could tell our story in a book,' Liam explained. 'It seemed no time at all before we got the call saying that it [*Forever Young*] had gone to Number One in the hardback book charts, which was unbelievable. It was only when we went to the signings and saw how many people were there, and how many people had bought the book that it all began to seem real.' Louis agreed: 'When we found out that *Forever Young* had got to Number One we were so shocked. We couldn't believe the size of the crowds who came along. Everywhere we looked there were massive crowds of people – it was so nice to be able to say thanks to everyone for supporting us.'

Though confessing that he found signing his autograph awkward as he hadn't practiced his penmanship, Harry was equally thrilled about the book: 'We were excited about it being out there and hoped that some fans would buy it, but we didn't realise just how many would get it,' Harry added. 'The fans that came along to the book signings were incredible. I got given lots of turtles because I once said I liked them – it's so cool when people remember little things you've said.'

CHAPTER EIGHT

UP ALL NIGHT

'Our aim with the album was to recreate the boy band
sound, and do something no one else is doing at the moment.
We didn't want to be sitting on stools and singing ballads
– we wanted some big songs that would surprise people.'
– Niall

On 11 September 2011, One Direction released their debut single 'What Makes You Beautiful', and those critics who'd churlishly mocked their performances on the X Factor Live Tour earlier in the year had to put away their poisoned pens when the single not only shot to the top of the UK chart – shifting just shy of 154,000 copies during the first week of release – but also broke Sony's existing pre-order record into the bargain.

Needless to say, the news that 'What Makes You Beautiful' had gone to the top of the download chart went down well with the boys families, as Louis's mum Johannah told her local newspaper, *The Star*: 'I was driving, picking up Louis's sisters, when we heard they were the download Number One. We were all just screaming! I tried to phone Louis but couldn't get hold of him until 7:10pm, because he's been so busy touring in a helicopter they had hired for [the] tour. He got mobbed by about four thousand people in Glasgow. When his sisters got on the school bus they got on to loads of cheers! Now we're keeping our fingers crossed that they're Number One in the chart this weekend.'

When the paper asked what the Tomlinson clan would be doing if – as expected – the single followed suit on the main chart, Johannah replied: 'We're going to have a party on Sunday night, with all the children, grandparents and Louis's great grandma, Olive Rothery. She's 89, but she knows all the words to their song already and sings along. She's learned about the internet to see what's on there about him.'

The paper was curious to know a little bit about their recent trip down to London to visit their celebrity son. 'We stayed at Louis and Harry's flat along with Harry's parents,' Johannah revealed. 'They only thing they had in to eat was cereal! They usually get home late and are too tired to cook. They seem to be having lots of fun and they're

giggling all the time. We're amazed by their fan base! Their fans have waited a year for them to get a record out, and I know the boys are really appreciative of that.'

The critics were forced to swallow an even bigger mouthful of humble pie when 'What Makes You Beautiful' became the highest *Billboard* Hot 100 debut for a UK act since Take That back in 1998, entering the chart at Number 28. Needless to say, One Direction's ever-increasing popularity ensured that 'What Makes You Beautiful' pipped Adele, Jessie J, and Ed Sheeran to scoop the award for Best British Single at the 2012 BRIT Awards. 'When we were recording in the studio we knew instantly that we wanted this track to be our first single,' Harry told *MTV News*. 'I think for us we wanted something that wasn't cheesy, but it was fun. It kind of represented us.' Liam added: 'We always wanted the single to be something people didn't expect and then when we heard it, it wasn't what we expected either so it kind of fitted perfectly.'

Up All Night, which was recorded in London, Los Angeles and Sweden, slammed onto the UK album chart at Number Two as the fastest-selling debut album of 2011, and was only kept off the prestigious top spot by Rihanna's *Talk That Talk*. But the boys did score a Number One hit in several countries around the world, including Australia, New Zealand, Canada, Sweden, Italy and Mexico.

Billboard magazine's Jason Lipshutz enthusiastically sang the album's praises: '*Up All Night* demonstrates an originality in sound that was necessary for the revitalisation of the boy band movement,' he raved. 'The electro pop currently dominating Top 40 radio is seamlessly weaved into the pop harmonies made standards by 'N Sync, Backstreet Boys

'When we were recording in the studio we knew instantly that we wanted "What Makes You Beautiful" to be our first single.' – Harry

and 98 Degrees – for instance, the title track sounds like a hybrid of Backstreet Boys' "Larger Than Life" and an LMFAO song, and even includes a Katy Perry name-check. *Up All Night* has its ups and downs, but One Direction complete two important tasks on their debut album: the boy band notches a long-lasting hit with "What Makes You Beautiful", and they look forward instead of back. Get ready to hear a lot more of One Direction.'

Following on from the aforementioned 'What Makes You Beautiful', and 'Gotta Be You', track three on the album is the equally upbeat, and perfectly executed 'One Thing', which allows Louis and Niall to show their respective solo skills. With its breezy synthesisers, 'More Than This' has what Jason Lipshutz described as a 'slower, Backstreet Boys feel', which showcases all the boys' voices more – notably Liam's falsetto range, while 'Up All Night' is an extremely catchy title number that bounces along before leaping into the booming chorus, which makes you want to 'Stay up all night and jump around'.

> 'We're not robots; we're just normal teenage lads who go through the same things as every other teenage lad.'
>
> – Harry

'I Wish', while undoubtedly one of the weaker tracks on the album, still boasts very impressive vocals. 'Tell Me A Lie' shows One Direction at their best and features another of Zayn's powerful solos, while the ballad-esque 'Taken' sees Liam and Harry serenade us about their troubles with a possessive ex-girlfriend who endeavours to get them back after realising they are 'taken'. 'We're not robots; we're just normal teenage lads who go through the same things as every other teenage lad,' Harry explained of the band's appeal on the Irish TV show *The Late Late Show* in November 2011.

'I Want' is arguably another 'filler' song, but the boys immediately get back on track with the infinitely more uplifting 'Everything About You', which again sees Niall and Louis take centre stage. 'Same Mistakes' is another sweeping ballad dedicated to the wily, yet irresistible fairer sex, which sees Harry and Zayn once again doing what they do best. 'The good thing about Simon [is that] he's always there when we need him, and we got a lot of freedom on [the album] and he wanted it to come more from us than from him so we got the choice of what went on the album,' Liam said on *The Late Late Show*. 'We co-wrote on some [songs] so, yeah, it was really nice to write the album and just have a little bit of freedom rather than being told what to do.'

'Save You Tonight' sees the boys approach the album's overriding boy-meets-girl theme by telling the object of their desire how they'll be their 'superhuman' who'll appreciate them more than anyone, which is sure to make a few boyfriends jealous if nothing else, as Harry explains: 'The reason why the fans are so dedicated is because I think they feel like they can really relate to us, like we're the kind of boys that you go to school with – and we are.' The album's final track, 'Stole My Heart', is another racy, up-tempo classic that explores the eternal notion of love at first sight – the perfect way to bring *Up All Night* to a close.

'We're really happy with how the album came out in the end. We took a lot of time over it because we wanted to make sure we got the right sound and stuff, so we didn't just kind of dive in and get a quick record out of it,' Liam told radio host Elvis Duran in March 2012. 'We wanted to make sure that we got a good record out of it. There's

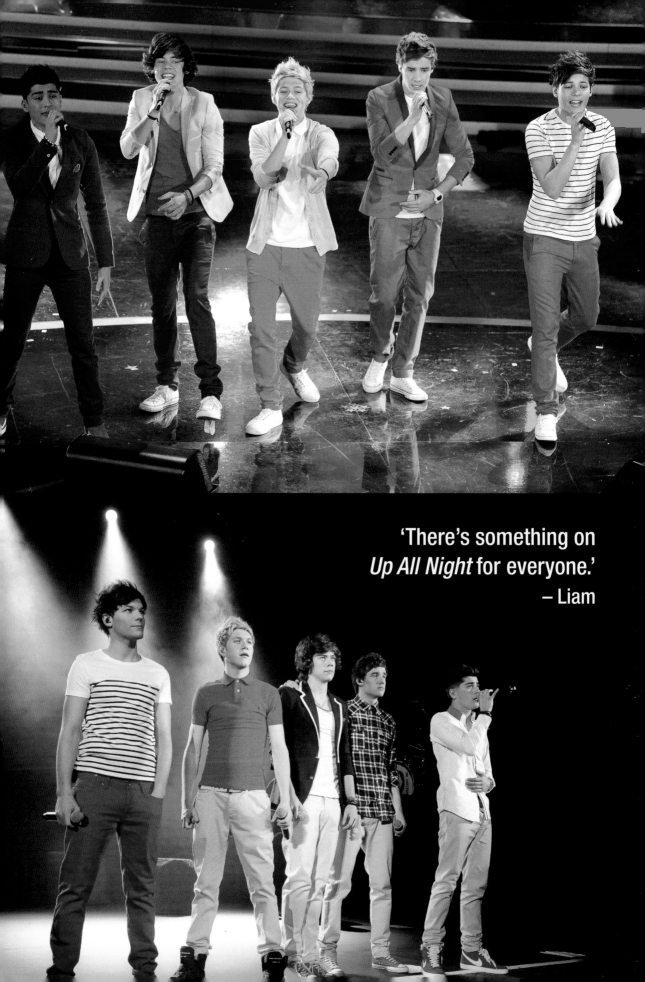

'There's something on
Up All Night for everyone.'
– Liam

something on there for everyone.' Niall concurred: 'We're pretty proud of the album that we have and hopefully it goes on to do big things.'

Though the boys undoubtedly found the recording process extremely hard work, they thoroughly enjoyed their time in the studio: 'Thankfully, we got lots of say in the [recording process],' Liam told the *Irish Times* 'We got to choose a lot of the songs and that sort of stuff. That was important to us with *X Factor*, too – we kind of put our own stamp on the boy band thing. Some of the time we actually sat there and there was no song – we came up with the concept from the beginning. Toby Gad was one of the guys we wrote with. He wrote "If I Were A Boy", which was obviously a massive song – so to work with someone like that when we're just starting off is a massive deal. If you think of someone like Justin Timberlake, who was in a boy band and came out of a boy band and is still making great music today – he's definitely someone who's dictated his career. He's written his own music and made his own songs and even signs artists, so he's someone to look up to, definitely.'

'Songwriting's a very precious thing, you know?' Zayn told the same paper. 'When you write your own music you can be quite precious about it, and it can be quite hard to express it to people. But we always felt comfortable. And we had each other to show

our ideas to.' Harry added: 'We have a lot of ideas that we share with our management and we actually get listened to a lot, believe it or not.'

Harry also shared his thoughts on the album's track-listing with the *Daily Mirror* in August 2011. Having let it be known that he and the rest of the boys had stood up to Simon and his Syco team, he said: 'Some of the lyrics were about 40-year-old men pouring their hearts out. I can't imagine ever being quite that old. We said "no" to at least one song, but he [Simon] would much prefer us to be honest. Despite what people think, he doesn't want to be surrounded by lots of "yes" men. We get quite a lot of freedom and a say in what we do. Once we found our sound, we told Simon we wanted to keep it really young. Simon wants us to put a stamp on our music, so he appreciates our input.'

While revealing how they'd 'enjoyed every minute of the writing and recording for the album', Liam admitted that they'd found the whole process of trying to find the perfect first single extremely nerve-wracking. 'We worked with some amazing writers and producers

> 'We're pretty proud of the album that we have and hopefully it goes on to do big things.'
> – Niall

'When you write your own music you can be quite precious about it, and it can be quite hard to express it to people. But we always felt comfortable.'
– Zayn

and it felt incredible to have these people on our side. We all got to do a lot of co-writing on the album, which was really important for us and we loved being involved. There are slow songs, up-tempo songs, some mid-tempo songs, there is something for everyone. A lot of the songs we recorded over the past months, and we thought people would enjoy them.'

'As soon as we started recording [the] music we were aware that people would be surprised by it, because it's not typical boy band music,' Zayn offered. 'There's nothing else out there like our sound at the moment. It's completely new. It's One Direction's sound and we love it.' Louis added: 'When we were in *X Factor* we absolutely loved being in the recording studio, so we were really excited about getting back in there. The studio is a great place to be because we get to hang out with each other, and we always get to order in good takeaways. As anyone who knows us will know, we like our food.'

To promote the album the boys embarked on their debut UK headline tour, which, following a 'rehearsal' show at the Watford Coliseum on 18 December 2011, got underway for real the following night at the Cliffs Pavilion in Westcliff-on-Sea. Many of the venues were rumoured to have sold out within seconds of the tickets going on sale, which led to further dates being added, as well as extra matinee performances at the existing venues. However, due to the boys' ever-increasing popularity, the tour was extended to include Australasia and North America, culminating with a show at Madison Square Garden in New York on 3 December 2012.

When reviewing their show at the Bournemouth International Centre, the *Observer*'s critic, Kitty Empire, remained largely unmoved by the boys' onstage efforts, likening them to 'lolloping foals let loose in the Men's department of H&M', and describing Harry – somewhat uncharitably – as a 'seventeen-year-old alpha puppy', before signing off with a cynical dig about how the only dance on show was 'one between group-conformity and future individuality'. The *Daily Mirror*'s James Robertson was rather more appreciative of the band's appearance at the HMV Hammersmith Apollo: 'The room shook with hair-raising, ear-drum-piercing and (if there had been windows) glass-shattering screams. Each took a turn walking forward to embrace the cries from the sold-out Hammersmith Apollo while singing the lame-named "Na Na Na". It was impossible to tell which one of the five boys had the biggest ovation, but the loudest cheer came when Niall played acoustic guitar as they sang solo around an artificial camp fire.'

'One Thing' was released as One Direction's third single in February 2012, midway through the tour. Perhaps because the track had already appeared on *Up All Night*, the single debuted at a rather desultory Number 28 on the UK chart and barely scraped into the Top Ten. However, though released only as a digital download in America, 'One Thing' reached a very respectable Number 62 on the *Billboard* Hot 100. The song's stateside success could have been due to them debuting 'One Thing' when they appeared on America's long-running breakfast TV show, the *Today Show*, and an estimated 15,000 fans gathered in the plaza outside the Rockefeller Centre in New York, from where the show is broadcast. It was one of the biggest audiences the show had pulled in for a live guest performance, with *Billboard* magazine's Steve Horowitz going so far as to declare it an 'unprecedented turnout for an act that had yet to release an album stateside'.

But of course, America hadn't seen anything yet . . .

CHAPTER NINE

THE ONLY WAY IS UP

'I don't know if I'll ever get used to fame. We've got more used to situations like going into a hotel and there being people there waiting for us, but surprising things happen all the time and you never really know what to expect – that's what makes it exciting.'
– Louis

Though it's often said that truth can be stranger than fiction, not even Simon Cowell could have foreseen the stateside reaction to One Direction. For while America has been driven to distraction by what's happening on the British music scene on previous occasions – most notably, of course, with the Beatles, who were forced to abandon touring the United States because of the hysteria which followed their every move – not even the Fab Four could boast having their debut album slam in at Number One on the *Billboard* chart. 'I couldn't be happier for One Direction, it is an incredible achievement,' Simon told the BBC. 'They deserve it. They have the best fans in the world.'

'We simply cannot believe that we are Number One in America,' Harry beamed. 'We want to thank each and every one of our fans in the US who bought our album and we would also like to thank the American public for being so supportive of us.' Niall added: 'As you can imagine, we are over the moon. When we got put together as a group, we couldn't imagine ourselves coming to America, let alone releasing our album here, so for us to be sitting at the top of the US album charts is unbelievable.' Liam was also quick to acknowledge his good fortune when giving a telephone interview to ITV's *Daybreak* after *Up All Night* entered the *Billboard* chart at Number One, by admitting that he and the other boys had been 'lucky' to have been singled out for One Direction. 'It's just really surreal to think you were one of those five lucky people. Anyone could have been chosen that day.'

During an interview with *Rolling Stone* while *Up All Night* was sitting pretty at the top of the US chart, Simon gave his thoughts on why the majority of British bands failed to make it in America simply because they tried to mimic their US counterparts, and ended up with a sound that sounded 'somewhere between England and America – which means you fall smack down in the middle of the ocean [as] you don't appeal to either.' He knew that for One Direction to have any hope of cracking the US market, they would have to have their own British sound, which would not only be something different, but also something they liked themselves. 'Every record we made and we progressed with, it was always based off the feedback from the boys in the studio,' he told the magazine. 'If they liked something, we went ahead. If they didn't like it, we threw it in the bin. They were a big part of the selection process of the songs on the record.'

Simon went on to echo *Music Week*'s Paul Williams by saying that he was surprised at the lack of bands in the current US charts compared with the 1990s, when New Kids On The Block, Backstreet Boys and 'N Sync held a monopoly on the airwaves. 'It's very much at the moment all about solo artists. Interestingly, you're seeing a lot of these artists collaborate with so many people and they're putting out seven or eight singles a year. So the charts become very track-led. Thank God kids love following an artist. When you get a group who pop, it's the best thing in the world. It's just been waiting to happen for years.'

> '**I couldn't be happier for One Direction, it is an incredible achievement. They deserve it. They have the best fans in the world.**'
> – Simon Cowell

Simon, of course, was well seasoned in how things work in the American music industry, but rather than 'hassle' the US labels as he had done previously, he decided to wait for them to make the first move: 'This time we said, "Let's just wait for the phone to ring and see who phones first,"' he told *Rolling Stone*. 'I wanted them to find out about the group first in a more buzzy way rather than us forcing the band on them. Rob Stringer [Columbia Records chairman] was the first person to call, and he said, "I really think we can break this band in America." I said, "It's going to take a little while." We wanted to put the record out in the UK and Europe. When I was out in America doing the auditions for *The X Factor*, everywhere I went there were blocks of One Direction fans going, "When are you going to bring this band to America?" I was going to put them on the final of *The X Factor* [USA] last year, but there was a conflict on the dates so they weren't able to do it. I was willing to take a chance on them even then, because I had a feeling they were going to make a big impact.'

He said he saw his job regarding One Direction's future was to make sure that Syco continued to encourage the best songwriters and producers to work with the boys and make the best possible records. 'As I said to them from day one, "You have to enjoy yourselves. You're going to make a lot of money, but you have to enjoy every single minute of it." When I see them now, they look fresh and they're having a good time. They know they can call me any time they have an issue. They have a fantastic relationship with management. It's been an absolute pleasure from day one to work with these guys.'

While it was this undoubtedly the immediate impact One Direction had on the *Billboard* chart that led to the media on both sides of the Atlantic making comparisons between One Direction and the Beatles, Louis wasn't getting too carried away and kept

'All these things that we get to do and the life that we get to have is just amazing. It's important that we never take that for granted.'

– Harry

his feet firmly planted on the ground: 'To be our generation's Beatles . . . wow. It is hugely flattering, but I'm not sure how seriously we can take it because it seems so unrealistic.'

'The fans over here are really loud and crazy,' Niall gasped. 'When we're in the tour bus, they [the fans] start climbing all over it and smacking on the windows, trying to get in. They start chasing after us, screaming. Coming out of the gig venue the other night was really difficult because these girls were everywhere. The traffic was heavy so they kept catching us up and following the bus. One girl was like an Olympic sprinter. She followed us for about five blocks to our hotel. She was unbelievably fit.'

'Since we've been out here, it's been crazy,' a beaming Harry told reporters. 'It seems to have blown up a bit, it's been insane for us, we're just riding the wave, working hard and having a lot of fun. When you're younger, America's this huge place where you go on holiday, and now we're working out here and doing shows, it's crazy. For us to even be here and have this kind of reaction is just incredible. People are being so, so nice and welcomed us so much, and for them to have taken the interest that they have in us feels pretty special. We're not really thinking too far ahead. It's all still sinking in, really. In Boston we did a meet-and-greet and these five girls came dressed as each of us. They do that a lot. It's cool.'

'We wouldn't have been able to get that Number One without the fans,' Louis added. 'We just can't thank them enough, because it was their work as much as ours.' Liam was equally bewildered: 'Our tour manager told us it would take three years of hard graft to do well in America . . . so for it to have taken off as it has is incredible,' he enthused. 'Twitter has been a major factor in getting our name out there in the States. Just as Twitter has gone up, so we have, too. For me it's a slow process, if you like, of dealing with girls screaming and telling me that they love me with tears rolling down their face. I've never seen anything like this before and, obviously, when I was going to school I never had six, seven hundred girls screaming at me everywhere I went.'

Though Simon had undoubtedly played a major role in establishing One Direction's profile in America, he readily agreed when *Rolling Stone* highlighted the importance of social networking sites such as Facebook and Twitter: 'For the music business, social networking is brilliant,' he told the magazine. 'Just when you think it's doom and gloom and you have to spend millions of pounds on marketing and this and that, you have this amazing thing now called fan power. The whole world is linked through a laptop. It's amazing. And it's free. I love it. It's absolutely brilliant.'

However, while eulogising about the benefits of social networking, he was quick to issue a caveat that it didn't guarantee success: 'But there's tons of groups out there. It doesn't happen to everyone. If you're good – and I've always believed this – and you're patient and the management is smart, it'll work perfectly. I'm not going to lie to you. I didn't sit here two years ago with some master plan. We just had five brilliantly talented people who I really liked. We made the best record we could, and we hoped for the best.

Louis, of course, had said as much on *One Direction: A Year In The Making*: 'Let's be honest, if we were around, say, ten years ago, people would have no idea who we are [outside the UK] because there wasn't Twitter; there wasn't YouTube; there was none of that. You come over to a country where you've done literally zero promotion and just through the power of the internet, that's why we've got such an amazing fan base out here.'

The boys latest US jaunt was supporting US boy band Big Time Rush on the latter's Better With U US Tour, but despite their superficial similarities, there was never any rivalry between the two bands. Indeed, according to Louis, the common ground between them made for a relaxed atmosphere, as the boys explained on Elvis Duran's 'must-hear' radio show: 'On the first show that we played with Big Time Rush, we were all so overwhelmed really by the support and how loud the crowd were,' Louis enthused. 'We all had planned out certain things that we wanted to get across in our talks and, actually, I was kind of lost for words 'cause we just didn't expect that kind of reaction and I didn't really prepare for it.' Niall added: 'Our biggest surprise on the tour was the amount of fans that sang our songs back to us. It was just crazy to think that . . . the number of people that knew who we were and knew our songs before the album even came out.'

Fans laid siege to the hotels where the boys were staying while out on the road with Big Time Rush, with the beleaguered NYPD being called out several times to control the crowds gathered outside the midtown Manhattan hotel where the boys were residing during their stay in New York (where they played the legendary Radio City Music Hall on Friday 9 March). Screaming swarms of Directioners descended anywhere and everywhere they might catch a glimpse of their idols, and many of these fans, of course, would have been thrilled on hearing the news that heartthrob Harry was a free agent again, after ending his much-publicised relationship with *XTRA Factor* host, Caroline Flack, who was fifteen years his senior.

Harry had first made his intentions towards Caroline known during the early rounds of *X Factor* by telling the show's official website that Caroline was 'gorgeous'. While nothing happened immediately, a couple of months later the two were spotted kissing at an *X Factor* party, and the not-so-secret romance became public knowledge the following month when they were photographed coming out of a West End restaurant. Since then the lovebirds had regularly stayed at each other's houses, and Caroline was even seen driving Harry to gigs.

It wasn't all plain sailing for Caroline, however, as the television beauty, once romantically linked to Prince Harry, was subjected to online abuse from One Direction fans over their relationship. She tweeted at the time: 'I'm close friends with Harry. He's one of the nicest people I know. I don't deserve death threats.' Yet while the split was supposed to be amicable, sources close to the band revealed that Harry had been under immense pressure to end the relationship, because of the possibility that the pair's age difference could damage One Direction's clean-cut image.

The couple's ill-fated romance had hit the headlines in January, and it was obvious to all that Harry still had feelings for Caroline, as in response to the tabloids' claims that he'd ended the relationship he tweeted: 'Please know I didn't "dump" caroline. This was a

'To be our generation's Beatles . . . wow.
It is hugely flattering, but I'm not sure how seriously we can take
it because it seems so unrealistic.'
– Louis

mutual decision. She is one of the kindest, sweetest people I know. Please respect that.'
However, it wasn't long before he was back in Caroline's arms, and speculation is again rife
as to whether this latest split will prove equally brief. 'There's a huge physical attraction
between them,' an insider said. 'It's made it hard for them to walk away from each other.'

While news of Harry's split from Caroline set the glossy gossip columnists' tongues
wagging, the news that Harry was expecting Louis's baby caused plenty of consternation
amongst their fans until it was realised that this 'bombshell' was nothing more than a
Louis-led April Fool prank – a prank aided and abetted by the *X Factor* camp, which
tweeted: 'We can confirm that @Harry Styles IS pregnant. If it's a girl he's calling it
Anne. If it's a boy, Juan Direction Styles. #HarrysPregnant.'

Louis had decided to play the prank in response to the news that an increasing
number of their American fans were convinced he and Harry were in a relationship
– despite the recent exposés over Harry's love life, and Louis being snapped out and
about in LA with his new girlfriend Eleanor Calder, a part-time model who'd just started
her second year at Manchester University studying politics and sociology. 'Some people

genuinely think that we're in a relationship,' Louis chuckled during an interview with Dallas radio station KXAS. 'I was looking at this thing the other day. They genuinely, seriously think that we're in a relationship. It's so funny!'

While Louis prefers to keep his private life exactly that, being one fifth of the most talked-about band in the world meant there was little likelihood of him keeping people in the dark about new flame Eleanor. And so it proved when the *Sun* broke the story – on 17 September 2011 – by saying how Eleanor had 'posed in her smalls for fashion firm Hollister in the kind of snaps wee Louis would have had plastered all over his bedroom walls', before his making it big on *The X Factor* allowed him to live an existence where his dream woman could become a reality.

According to the *Sun*'s intrepid showbiz column, a pal of Louis's had revealed that 'Louis can't believe his luck. He is in awe of how fit she [Eleanor] is. They went to see *The Inbetweeners Movie* together the other day and they've been out for a few secret dates. He's getting stuck in. She is a couple of years older than him but the lads in the band think she's the female version of Louis. She is gobby, loud and confident but pretty laidback at the same time. She isn't afraid to bend the rules either – just like Louis. It looks like she could be serious girlfriend material.'

> 'It seems to have blown up a bit, it's been insane for us, we're just riding the wave, working hard and having a lot of fun.'
> – Harry

On 13 March an estimated three thousand teenagers descended on the Stonebriar Centre Mall in Frisco, Texas – situated some 25 miles outside of Dallas – to grab a copy of *Up All Night*, and get a chance to get up close and personal with the boys. The first 1,000 people through the door who purchased the album at the mall's Barnes & Noble store that day would be guaranteed a wristband that would give them access to an autograph event and performance at the Dr. Pepper Ballpark in Dallas eleven days later on 24 March.

While there were conflicting reports as to whether or not the number of kids who got their hands on a wristband was doubled due to popular demand, trouble flared amongst the 1,000 or so who didn't get one of the much-coveted wristbands. According to local TV network KDWF-TV, scores of fans were left battered and bruised following a frenzied stampede the moment the mall opened its doors, and at least one fan was hospitalised for breathing problems.

'It's been a very long time since a music group has debuted to cause this kind of fan hysteria and excitement in the United States,' the *Metro* explained. 'Most of the acts from *The X Factor* have not made it big in America, so it has been truly extraordinary for One Direction to be such an instant smash in every country where its music is on sale.'

The boys' management were obviously anxious to avoid a repeat performance of the chaotic scenes at the Stonebriar book store as, according to the *Daily Mail*, they arrived at the Dr. Pepper Ballpark flanked by a team of security guards: 'They're arguably the biggest boy band at the moment, so the fans are obviously bound to be hyped up,' the paper declared. 'But One Direction's management could be being a little over-

protective on their US tour as the boys will reportedly have twenty bodyguards each during their stay in Dallas.'

Sources said that a security team of 100 had been assigned to protect the group for their performance in Dallas, which is only supposed to last 45 minutes. They were scheduled to play just four songs for a crowd of about 7,000 at the Dr. Pepper Ballpark. And the boys could have some pretty high-profile guests at their gig. It was revealed last week that Niall Horan had been tweeting American TV personality Khloe Kardashian to invite her as she lives in Dallas. The blond pop singer wrote to the reality star: 'Hey khloe, we are coming to dallas next week for a fan event performing and stuff ! you and lemar should come along!'

> 'We wouldn't have been able to get that Number One without the fans. We just can't thank them enough, because it was their work as much as ours.'
> – Louis

On Saturday, 31 March 2012, One Direction performed at Nickelodeon's 25th Annual Kids' Choice Awards, which honours children's favourite music, television, film and pop culture acts, with celebrities often getting 'slimed' with a gooey green substance on stage. The awards show, hosted by Will Smith, was held at the USC Galen Centre in Los Angeles and included guest appearances by luminaries such as America's First Lady,

Michelle Obama, and the actors Robert Downey Jr., Halle Berry, and *Hunger Games* star Josh Hutcherson. And while the boys weren't listed amongst the nominations for 'Favourite Music Group', the award was won by their pals Big Time Rush.

Once again, they would be performing 'What Makes You Beautiful', but unlike previous stateside performances of their debut single, the boys promised a 'special surprise' for their fans, as Harry explained: 'We've done the song on a few different shows now, so we just wanted to make this one as big as possible, and surprise the fans with the performance side of things. We've got a big production and we want to get the audience involved with us.' During the show, huge white balloons were dropped into the crowd, and celebrities including Taylor Swift, Katy Perry and Selena Gomez could be seen dancing in the audience.

While the boys were en route to Australasia, where they could expect an equally rapturous welcome, little did they know that lawyers acting for a hitherto unknown Californian band were preparing to drop a bombshell in their lap, as the *Guardian* reported on 11 April 2012: 'Simon Cowell's boy band One Direction, among the hottest new acts in the music business, has been sued for trademark infringement because it is using the same name as a small California pop-rock group.'

Speaking to the BBC's *Newsbeat* in their first UK broadcast interview, the five-piece

'Our fans are simply the best in the world. The support they have shown us has been incredible and we're all so grateful to each and every one of them.'
– Niall

Californian outfit's eighteen-year-old singer, Sean O'Leary, said that while he and the rest of the band had received death threats and hate mail over the row, they wouldn't be backing down from the $1 million (£630,000) lawsuit. 'He [Simon] is obviously a very smart man, but we are not intimidated,' O'Leary said. 'The law isn't a popularity contest. Our name has been infringed. When I was small and tried to start things up, my dad would always advise me you're at the bottom so there's only one direction to go. And that was the attitude I needed for the band.'

While Syco remained tight-lipped about the lawsuit, Harry and Zayn went before the Australian press to say that, while they had no idea what was going on behind the scenes, they were adamant that they wouldn't be changing their name – as were Niall, Liam and Louis. And closer to home, in an interview with the *Sun*, Niall's dad Bobby told the paper: 'I want my boy and the rest of the group to keep touring under their name. They've worked hard to sell records under that name. They have cracked the States and that's the way it should stay.'

After telling the paper about what he's had to put up with when dealing with the more extreme One Direction fans who show up uninvited at his home, or those who mail things to him, such as underwear for Niall to autograph, Bobby said that while he was very proud of the success Niall had achieved with One Direction, he wouldn't be one of those parents expecting handouts from their famous offspring. 'I don't want one penny of Niall's money. He's offered me big things like a car but I've always said no. I'm happy living and working as I am. I've been a butcher most of my life and I'm going to keep doing that until I retire. I laughed when I saw him [in the newspapers] and the lads enjoying themselves on a yacht in Australia. He's gone in completely the opposite direction of my life, and I love watching it happen.'

Just as they had in the UK, tickets for the five Australasian shows had sold out within minutes of going on sale. Indeed, such was the 1D euphoria down under that the *Melbourne Herald Sun* couldn't help but get caught up in the hysteria when the boys performed at the city's Hisense Arena on 16 April. Having eulogised One Direction as being a 'cleverly cast pop band with plenty of personality unleashed at the perfect time and seizing their moment', the paper then praised the boys for taking time out between numbers to respond to the questions tweeted by the audience. 'They say, wear and sing all the right things to connect directly with their pocket-money demographic,' the paper enthused. 'Throw in their own tweeting and it creates an access and ownership that explains why they've captured teen hearts so fast.'

Of course, it was at the Hisense Arena that the boys were reacquainted with their old *X Factor* pal Dannii Minogue. Despite her personal upheavals following her recent split from boyfriend Kris Smith, and the equally-recent tabloid revelations about her affair with Simon Cowell, Dannii put on a brave face to come along and applaud the boys for what they'd achieved since she'd last been in the same room with them at *The X Factor* final, when the boys had been fighting back the tears, thinking their journey was at an end – and now here they were, playing to hordes of screaming teenage girls. According to sources, Dannii told the boys how proud she was of them, and that she'd loved the gig.

At the time of writing, One Direction have completed their sold-out, five-date tour of Australasia, and will take a month-long break to recharge their batteries, as well as spend some of the whopping £10 million pay-out they've reportedly just received from Syco, before kick-starting the *Up All Night* Tour's 25-date North American leg – which also includes dates in Canada and Mexico – at the Patriot Centre in Fairfax, Virginia, on 24 May.

The boys' 2013 diary is already looking pretty busy, with further sell-out tours of the UK, Australasia and North America. They had initially announced fifteen dates across the UK and Ireland, but were once again forced to add extra dates and matinee shows – including six sold-out dates at London's O2 Arena. And how many bands can pull that kind of crowd? Following the announcement that One Direction would be extending the 2013 tour to include North American and Australasian legs, an excited Niall told *MTV News*: 'Our fans are simply the best in the world. The support they have shown us has been incredible and we're all so grateful to each and every one of them.'

While One Direction will always have their detractors, it's worth remembering that they weren't the ones shouting about being the new Beatles, the new Take That, or the new anything. After all, the very nature of pop music means that it will be periodically rehashed and repackaged – and right now the name on the cover of every schoolgirl's exercise book is One Direction. 'We're not trying to be anything that we're not,' Liam said on Elvis Duran's *Morning Show*. 'We're just trying to be ourselves, have a good time . . . and I think that's what people enjoy.'

British Library Cataloguing in Publication Data

O'Shea, Mick.
One Direction: no limits.
1. One Direction (Musical group)–Juvenile literature.
I. Title
782.4'2164'0922-dc23

ISBN-13: 978-085965-493-7

Cover photo by IBL/Rex Features
Cover and book design by Coco Wake-Porter
Printed in Great Britain by Scotprint

Acknowledgements

Professional thanks to Sandra Wake, Laura Slater and Tom
Branton at Plexus for their assistance in my bringing the
book in on time, Rupert Tracy, and Jackie and Richard @
P-PR. Thanks also to Tasha 'Stash' Cowen and Shannon
'Mini-Hepburn' Stanley, for again putting up with my
mood-swings and frustrations when I occasionally
stumbled over the dreaded writer's block, Paul Young
(not the singer), Lisa 'T-bag' Bird, Zoe Johnson-Meadows,
Sarah 'the Angel Lady', Martin and Angela Jones, Phil and
Nic Williams, Sharon Hilton and Simon Godfrey.

The members of One Direction have given
innumerable interviews to newspapers, magazines,
websites, television and radio. The author and editors
would like to thank: www.xfactor.itv.com, *XTRA Factor,
One Direction: Dare To Dream, One Direction:
Forever Young, One Direction A-Z, One Way Street: One
Direction, Teen Now* magazine, *The Star* (Doncaster
newspaper), *The Doncaster Free Press, The Bradford
Telegraph & Argus, One Direction: A Year In The
Making, The Wolverhampton Express & Star, Now*
magazine, *The Irish Herald, The Belfast Telegraph,* MSN
UK, *The Westmeath Examiner, The Crewe Chronicle,
Mizz* magazine, *The Mirror,* fanpop.com, *Rolling Stone*
magazine, *The Daily Telegraph, Digitalspy.com, The
Star, Sugarscape, The Guardian,* NME, *MTV News,
Trash Lounge, Billboard* magazine, *The Late, Late Show,
The Elvis Duran Morning Show, The Irish Times, The
Observer, Irish Evening Herald, The Today Show,* BBC
News, *Daybreak, Music Week, In:Demand,* BBC Radio
One, KXAS Radio, *The Daily Mail, The Sun, Metro,* BBC
Newsbeat, and *The Melbourne Herald Sun.*

We would also like to thank the following agencies
for supplying photographs: FilmMagic/ Fred Duval/ Getty
Images; FilmMagic/ Jon Kopaloff/ Getty Images; Jason
Sheldon/ Rex Features; Martin Karius/ Rex Features; IBL/
Rex Features; Fairfax Media via Getty Images; WireImage/
Mike Marsland/ Getty Images; Getty Images for KCA/
Christopher Polk; TOURE Cheick/ Rex Features; Matt
Baron/ BEI/ Rex Features; Beretta/ Sims/ Rex Features;
IBL/ Rex Features; Brian Rasic/ Rex Features; Beretta/
Sims/ Rex Features; Ken McKay/ Rex Features; Matt
Baron/ BEI/ Rex Features; Erik Pendzich/ Rex Features;
Beretta/ Sims/ Rex Features; IBL/Rex Features; Fairfax
Media/ Getty Images; FilmMagic/ Neil Mockford/ Stringer/
Getty Images; WireImage/ Jon Furniss/ Getty Images;
Steve Meddle/ Rex Features; WireImage/ Jon Furniss/
Getty Images; waynehowes/ Shutterstock.com; IBL/ Rex
Features; Fairfax Media via Getty Images; Picture Perfect/
Rex Features; Beretta/ Sims/ Rex Features; TOURE
Cheick/ Rex Features; Beretta/ Sims/ Rex Features; IBL/
Rex Features; Beretta/ Sims/ Rex Features; WireImage/
Jon Furniss/ Getty Images; FilmMagic/ Neil Mockford/
Stringer / Getty Images; Getty Images/ Neilson Barnard/
Stringer; Featureflash/ Shutterstock.com; MediaPunch/
Rex Features; WireImage/ JAB Promotions/ Getty Images;
FilmMagic/ Danny Martindale/ Getty Images; McPix Ltd/
Rex Features; Beretta/ Sims/ Rex Features; Beretta/ Sims/
Rex Features; Beretta/ Sims/ Rex Features; Getty Images/
Dave Hogan; Jonathan Hordle/ Rex Features; McPix Ltd/
Rex Features; McPix Ltd/ Rex Features; Newspix/ Rex
Features; WireImage/ Danny Martindale/ Getty Images;
Getty Images/ Ian Gavan/ Stringer/ Getty Images; Steve
Meddle/ Rex Features; Shropshire Star/ NTI Media
Ltd/ Rex Features; Matt Baron/ BEI/ Rex Features;
Newspix/ Rex Features; WireImage/ Shirlaine Forrest/
Getty Images; Billl McCay/ Getty Images; Newspix/ Rex
Features; FilmMagic/ SAV/ Getty Images; WireImage/ Jon
Furniss/ Getty Images; WireImage/ Jon Furniss/ Getty
Images; Getty Images/ Venturelli; FilmMagic/ Joseph
Okpako/ Getty Images; Getty Images/ Danny Martindale;
Getty Images/ Mathis Wienand; WireImage/ Jon Furniss/
Getty Images; Newspix/ Rex Features; Featureflash/
Shutterstock.com; Picture Perfect/ Rex Features; Picture
Perfect/ Rex Features; David Rowland/ Rex Features;
WireImage/ JesseGrant/ Getty Images; WireImage/
Michael Buckner/ Getty Images; WireImage/ George
Pimentel/ Getty Images; Newspix/ Nathan Richter/ Rex
Features; Simon Runting/ Stephen D'Antal/ Rex Features;
McPix Ltd/ Rex Features; MediaPunch/ Rex Features;
MediaPunch/ Rex Features; IBL/ Rex Features.